Smoke, Fire and Angels

To Cammy,

Thank you for your
help + being Joe's
aunt!

Mark Rd

Smoke, Fire and Angels

Tragedy on Avon Mountain and the Life-Changing Aftermath

Mark Robinson

All book proceeds will be donated to a fund to help those most seriously affected by the crash.

SMOKE, FIRE AND ANGELS

Mark Robinson

All book proceeds will go to a fund to help those most
seriously affected by the Avon Mountain tragedy of July 29, 2005.
To purchase books, make a donation or contact the author,
please visit: **www.smokefireandangels.com**

SPECIAL THANKS TO

ING

Duncan Somerville

Stan and Nancy McKenney

Bob Switzgable
Ski Sundown, New Hartford, Conn.

————

For their generosity toward the
production of this book,
thank you to

Wolf ColorPrint, Newington, Conn.

Hudson Valley Paper Company, Windsor Locks, Conn.

Connecticut Valley Bindery, New Britain, Conn.

PROJECT TEAM

PUBLISHED BY
Avon Mountain Angels Publishing
Canton, Connecticut

EDITORS
Chris John Amorosino   Beth Bruno
Howard Drescher   Nancy Simonds

PHOTOGRAPHY
John Muldoon
Avon Police and Fire Departments

DESIGN
Mary Crombie

MARKETING, MEDIA, PUBLIC RELATIONS
Chris John Amorosino   Linda "LB" Biancalani   Elizabeth Cowles
Jeff Dornenburg   Howard Drescher   Darcy O'Connor
Jeff Paine   Christine Robinson

WEBSITE
Sue Apito   Eric Tully   Richard Wilton

VIDEO
Michelle Leibovitz   Rich Wright

MAILING SERVICES
Barbara Barry

AUTHOR'S NOTE:
The people listed here gave their time, energy and creativity to the
Smoke, Fire and Angels *fundraising project. I deeply appreciate their help.*
Please see Resources on page 160 to contact them for their professional services.
In addition to being highly accomplished in their fields, they are great people!

DEDICATION

This book is dedicated to the memory of those
who died in the Avon Mountain tragedy,
to their grieving families and friends,
and to the rescuers who freed,
comforted and cared for those of us
who so desperately needed them.

And also to my wife, Chris, and son, Matt,
and all my family and friends for
taking care of me and supporting me
through this journey.

And finally,
in loving memory of my parents,
Kenneth and Eleanor Robinson

CONTENTS

What Makes the Avon Mountain
Crash Different?

The number is mind numbing – 43,443 people killed on U.S. road-ways in 2005. Picture a standing-room-only crowd at Boston's Fenway Park, and you'll still be 6,000 short. So what's one crash with a few fatali-ties? What makes the Avon Mountain crash different? Nothing, from one perspective. Nothing, because people die in crashes every day in every part of the country. Most attract little attention. Our eyes skim over the few inches of newsprint chronicling the latest carnage. After all, tens of thousands of deaths are almost beyond comprehension; we simply can-not get our minds or hearts around the reality of all those lives lost. Five people died as a result of the July 29, 2005 crash, accounting for only one one-hundredth of one percent of the traffic fatalities that year. In the over-all nationwide body count, the Avon Mountain crash was barely a blip.

But there is another answer to what makes this crash different: Everything. Everything, because someone's precious daddy/husband/mom/sister/fiancée/brother/daughter/son/teacher/friend left for work that day and never came home again. Everything, because the loss of those five lives is a harsh reminder that it can happen to anyone at any time, that every one of those 43,443 deaths in 2005 was a tragedy that dev-astated the loved ones left behind. Everything, because it was spectacular – the crash itself, the rescue effort, the irresponsibility that caused it. And everything, because "No man is an island," as the poet wrote, and "Each man's death diminishes me...therefore, send not to know for whom the bell tolls, it tolls for thee."[1]

There's one more reason why, at least for me, this crash was different: I was in it. There was nothing between me and the fully loaded, out-of-control Mack dump truck as I sat trapped and frozen in the front row of traffic. People in cars to my left, right and rear were killed. Why was I spared? Writing this book, in one sense, has been my attempt to deal with that question. There are several possible answers, one of which I can offer right up front: Maybe, just maybe, I was spared to write this book, to tell the amazing, heart-rending story of the Avon Mountain crash, the story of human beings suddenly confronted with catastrophe – the utterly random twists of fate that brought them to the point of impact; how they

---

1. John Donne, Meditation XVII

survived or died; how they took care of each other; how they carry on; and, for some, how they are remembered.

If this were a typical movie script, I'd need to narrow the focus to only a few main characters: a hero, a villain and maybe a handful of supporting cast members. But to do justice to the Avon Mountain story, you must know more. You must know about the heroism and humanity of the rescuers, the cold carelessness of those responsible for the crash, the courage and grace of the victims and their families. And most of all, you need to know the people at the center of this tragedy – the beloved special education teacher, a heroic, fairy-tale giant in the eyes of his special "elves"; the bus driver and his sacred promise to his daughter; two amazingly loving mothers; the drifter who was trying to turn his life around; the hard-edged truck owner who set the tragic chain of events in motion; the dentist from Belarus and the angels who saved her.

I could go on and on. And I do in the pages that follow. Please be patient as I introduce you to the people whose lives were on the line July 29, 2005, and the people who came to their rescue. And please indulge me in Chapter 1 as I set the context for this story and introduce you to me, your very-lucky-to-be-alive author.

INTRODUCTION

Good morning.

A few questions to ponder as you start your day:

- ✧ Will this be the day you die?
- ✧ Will this be the day someone you love walks out the door and never comes home again?
- ✧ Will this be the day your most mundane decisions – stop for coffee, change lanes, take the scenic route – will make the difference between life and death?
- ✧ Will this be the day your actions lead to another person's death?
- ✧ Will this be the day you are rendered utterly helpless, completely at the mercy of forces beyond yourself?
- ✧ Will this be the day when, ready or not, you are confronted with life's most difficult questions?
- ✧ Will this be the day your life changes forever?

For some of us stopped at a traffic light one morning in Connecticut's Farmington River Valley, July 29, 2005 was that day. It was a beautiful summer Friday. Most of us were doing what we do hundreds of times a year: simply going to work. There was no way to know what was coming as we approached the traffic light at the base of Avon Mountain and the intersection, the intersection of Nod Road and Routes 44 and 10, of chance and fate, of wrong place and wrong time.

This is a true story about real people, the best and the most irresponsible among us. It's about what happened before, during and after one of the worst crashes in Connecticut history. It's about innocent victims and heroes – everyday people who did extraordinary things, literally picking up the pieces of the broken lives left in the wake of a poorly maintained, uninsured, fully loaded, out-of-control Mack dump truck.

I don't remember anything about the fiery crash. I do know I'm lucky. Five people died, many were injured. I broke nine bones, punctured a lung and got my first helicopter ride. I was on the receiving end of amazing courage and kindness, came face to face with death and was, for some unfathomable reason, granted a reprieve.

As I began this journey to fill in the blanks of what happened that day, I wasn't sure what I'd find. I did know it was something I had to do. Because for some of us waiting at that intersection at the base of Avon Mountain, life would never be the same.

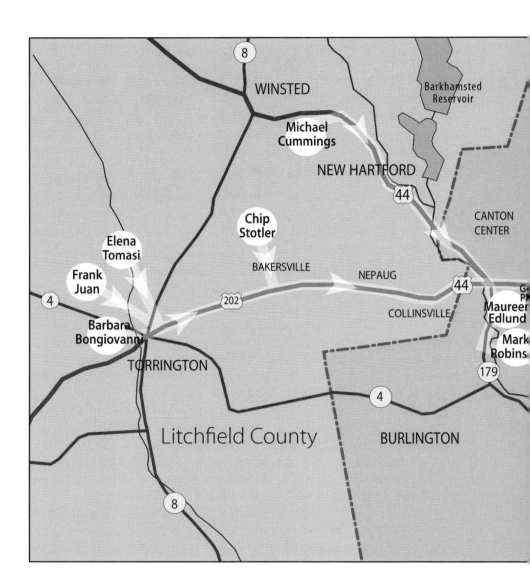

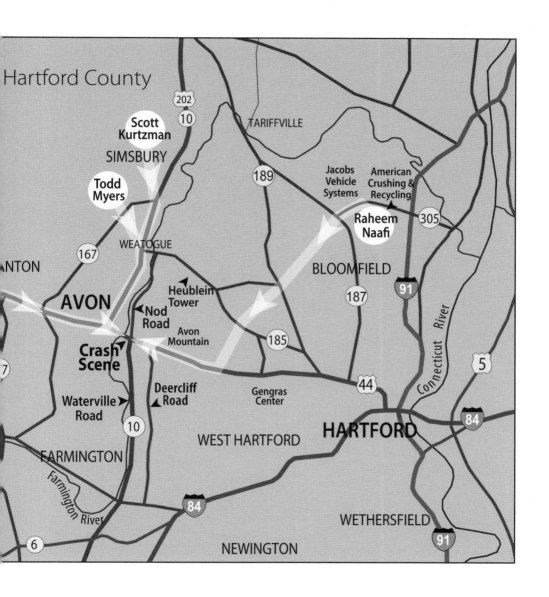

Hartford County

202
10
TARIFFVILLE

Scott
Kurtzman

SIMSBURY

189

Jacobs
Vehicle
Systems

American
Crushing &
Recycling

305

Todd
Myers

Raheem
Naafi

167

WEATOGUE

BLOOMFIELD

91

ANTON

AVON

Heublein
Tower

187

Nod
Road

Avon
Mountain

185

Connecticut River

5

7

Crash
Scene

Waterville
Road

Deercliff
Road

Gengras
Center

44

HARTFORD

84

10

WEST HARTFORD

FARMINGTON

Farmington River

84

WETHERSFIELD

91

6

NEWINGTON

PART 1

The Crash

CHAPTER 1

My New Commute

The day began like so many others. I had already taken Dixie, our lovable Lab/pit bull mutt, for her morning romp down by the river. I made strawberry-banana shakes for my wife Chris and me. We had a little spat the night before, no big deal, but I left that morning without saying goodbye. I got into my 2001 black Mercury Cougar and hurried toward Hartford. It was about 7:15 on Friday, July 29, 2005, a picture-perfect, sunny summer morning in Connecticut's Farmington River Valley. But I wasn't thinking about the weather. And I wasn't thinking about the weekend. I was thinking about a meeting scheduled to take place in Atlanta the following week.

I'm a director of internal communications for the U.S. division of Amsterdam-based ING, one of the world's largest financial services companies. We were preparing for the annual conference of top U.S. leaders. I had a long to-do list, and it all had to get done fast, and done right. No screwups, no surprises, no excuses. Dozens of questions ran through my mind: Did the corporate brand people make final changes to their PowerPoint presentation? Had the lawyers signed off on the panel discussion outline? Was my deadline to get all the drafts to the CEO for his weekend review 6:00 or 6:30 p.m.?

I should have left an hour earlier, I scolded myself, as I drove east on Route 44. Each red light and every lumbering bus or truck that got between me and my to-do list was ratcheting up my internal stress meter another notch or two. The radio was my only distraction. I was within a year of my 50th birthday, but my reflexes were still quick enough to change stations no more than two syllables into a Bob's Furniture commercial.

Two months ago, Chris and I had moved seven miles west from Farmington to Canton. That meant a new commute. I was now taking Route 44 through Avon into Hartford instead of the traffic-clogged Route 4 through Farmington – a big improvement, I thought. But Route 44, the main traffic artery between the Farmington Valley and Hartford, was no bargain either.

Several years earlier, I had worked at Security-Connecticut Life (SCL) Insurance Company in Avon. When ING announced in 2000 that it was going to acquire our parent company, ReliaStar, and also Aetna Financial Services in Hartford, most SCL employees were not happy. Many immediately speculated that ING would cut staff, close the Avon office and move the remaining jobs to Hartford. And that, many feared, would mean driving on that steep, narrow, twisting, unforgiving, accident-plagued section of Route 44 over Avon Mountain.

For the eastbound driver, Avon Mountain is a beautiful but forbidding barrier, rising suddenly from the valley floor. Green with summer foliage, it looks benign and peaceful in the morning light, as it has for many millenia. It is an incredibly ancient feature of Connecticut's landscape. Four hundred million years ago, the story of Avon Mountain started with a massive collision and intense fire. All of the continents had been drifting toward each other, ultimately colliding and forming a supercontinent. What we now call Connecticut was wedged between Africa and North America.

The supercontinent began to break apart two hundred million years later. Water flowed into the ever-widening gap, forming the Atlantic Ocean. Pressure from the newly separated land masses cracked the North American surface, creating faults from Newfoundland to Florida. One series of faults emerged through the center of Connecticut. Eventually, the deepening faults provided openings through which 2000-degree lava flowed, burning everything in its path. It cooled, forming dark, dense traprock.[1] Then more lava and more cooling. After several geological cycles, the fault stabilized into the backbone of the state, the Metacomet Ridge, stretching 70 miles from Long Island Sound all the way into Massachusetts.

On a clear day like July 29, 2005, hikers who climbed the ridge and the 120 steps to the top of Heublein Tower, perched 700 feet above the Farmington Valley in nearby Simsbury, could see "5,000 square-mile panoramic views that stretch into Rhode Island, Massachusetts and New York."[2] It was breathtaking views like these that lured developers to the ridge to build modern-day palaces for the particularly well-heeled, who along with many others were flooding into the Farmington Valley. The overall population grew steadily. The affluent town of Avon, for example, more than doubled in size, from about 8,000 in 1970 to 17,000 in 2005, when it was named the third safest town in America by *Money* magazine. Hundreds of millions of years in the making, it took only a fraction of a heartbeat in time to pockmark the pristine ridge with today's mega mansions.

The home under construction at 147 Deercliff Road was a "spec" house, meaning the builder was speculating that he'd eventually find a buyer. According to the real estate ad, the massive house would offer "magnificent western views, extraordinary style and design...a private sanctuary done in grand scale, all the high tech systems with classic details, spectacular appointments, shingle and stone country estate home – a masterpiece." With six bedrooms, eight full bathrooms and 13 acres, the 10,000-square-foot mansion could be yours for an asking price of $3.6 million.

At the high end of the market, 147 Deercliff was one of thousands of new homes built in the Farmington Valley area during the previous decade. All of those new homeowners put a strain on existing infrastructure, especially

---

1. Diana V. Wetherell, *Traprock Ridges of Connecticut: A Naturalist's Guide*
2. *Seasons of the Farmington Valley*, Spring 2007

roads like Route 44, or "Albany Turnpike" as it was called in the early 1800s, when tolls ranged from "one cent for each sheep or swine to twenty-five cents for a traveling four-wheeled pleasure carriage and horses."[3]

In more recent times, people came to the Farmington Valley because of its proximity to Hartford, "the insurance capital of the world." Companies such as ING, Aetna, The Hartford, United Health Care, CIGNA and The Travelers had large offices in Hartford, in addition to *Fortune 500* giant, United Technologies. People look to the suburbs for "quality of life" features like good schools, safe neighborhoods and great recreation. The picturesque valley had everything from hiking, biking, golf and fly fishing to kayaking and skiing. Or you could simply enjoy the natural beauty of the ridge, river and surrounding forests brimming with deer, dozens of species of birds and a growing population of black bears, coyotes, bobcats and foxes. Within about a two hour's drive were New York City, Boston, the mountains of Vermont and New Hampshire, and the ocean shorelines of Rhode Island and Massachusetts.

By 2005, some 23,000 vehicles a day were steadily trickling in from the back roads of towns like New Hartford, Simsbury and Canton, feeding the commuter torrent that had become Route 44 at rush hour. And it wasn't just commuters. Shoppers shared the crowded roads in ever-increasing numbers. The popularity of the valley had spawned a virulent strain of "mall sprawl" along the commuter corridor. That commerce required a daily influx of big trucks to stock the stores and to haul building material for all those new houses like the one rising at 147 Deercliff, just off Route 44 at the top of Avon Mountain.

Wussies. That's what I thought to myself when I heard my Security-Connecticut Life colleagues talk about how dangerous it was to drive Avon Mountain. Maybe it was a little tricky, but as Security-Connecticut Life CEO Jim Gelder tried to reassure everyone, it was only nine miles from our Avon headquarters to Hartford's Aetna-ING building. Only nine miles.

In fact, I may have been the only SCL employee who was happy about the ING merger news. As long as I survived the corporate "downsizing" that almost inevitably follows a major merger, my commute would be much shorter. Sure, I'd miss the family-like atmosphere we enjoyed in the comfortable and scenic setting of the SCL campus in Avon. Many of us probably didn't realize just how much we would miss it. But I wasn't going to miss that long commute. Back then, I lived in Mansfield, just down the road from the University of Connecticut (Go Huskies!) 30 miles *east* of Hartford. As a single dad, I made that 80-mile round-trip to Avon and back every day so my skateboarding, hockey-goalie son, Matt, could continue his education and sports activities in familiar surroundings. Relocating the SCL office from Avon to Hartford would cut almost an hour from my daily roundtrip commute.

3. Mary-Frances L. MacKie, *Avon, Connecticut*

And don't tell me about risky roads, I thought. After all, I had driven "Suicide 6" east of the Connecticut River for many years. Named by *Reader's Digest* and NBC's *Dateline* as one of the nation's most dangerous roads, an average of at least two people a year over several decades were killed on the 11-mile stretch of Route 6 from Windham through Bolton Notch. As was the case with fixing other dangerous Connecticut roads, the state dawdled while people died. So I knew all about dodging and weaving my way to work every day.

After Matt graduated from E.O. Smith High School, he was off to school in Massachusetts and Florida. Soon after, I met Chris and my life shifted to west of the Connecticut River. We married, and I moved to her place in Farmington. Almost a year later, in May 2005, we moved to Canton. That's when I began driving to Hartford on Route 44 over Avon Mountain, precisely the route that frightened many of my SCL colleagues.

But I wasn't worried about Route 44. After all, besides my experience dealing with Suicide 6, I had fond memories of a special event that had taken place near a major Route 44 intersection. A year earlier, Chris and I had our wedding reception at Avon Old Farms Inn at the base of Avon Mountain. It was one of the happiest days of my life. Matt was my Best Man. I confess that had made me just a bit nervous. Considering the cache of embarrassing material he had gathered on me during his 19 years, giving him the microphone in front of 125 family members and friends was. . . well, let's just say I had reason to be nervous. But like just about everything on that special day, Matt was great. He handled his Best Man responsibilities with poise and just the right touch of humor. For me, it was like seeing my son almost instantly transformed from a goofy kid with braces to a man. I was so proud of him.

And then there was Chris. There has never been a more beautiful bride. Her smile radiated throughout the reception hall and made me feel like the luckiest guy in the world. I was sure I was dreaming as we danced our first dance to the sultry sounds of Dusty Springfield's "The Look of Love."

Only one thing could have made June 12, 2004 any better. On June 12, 1949, fifty-five years earlier, my wonderful parents, Ken and Ellie Robinson, were married. They died in 2003 – my mom of leukemia on Mother's Day, May 11, and my dad of a broken heart on September 4. To honor them on our wedding day and to continue to keep them in our hearts, we displayed their wedding pictures just off the dance floor. Someone told me my parents were watching over us.

The light at the base of Avon Mountain turned red as I approached it that summer morning in July 2005. While waiting for it to turn green, I may have looked across the intersection over at Avon Old Farms Inn, as I sometimes did when stopped at the light, and smiled at the thought of that happy day not so long ago.

CHAPTER 2

Master in the Art of Living

The master in the art of living makes little distinction between his work and his play, his labor and his leisure, his mind and his body, his information and his recreation, his love and his religion. He hardly knows which is which. He simply pursues his vision of excellence at whatever he does, leaving others to decide whether he is working or playing. To him he's always doing both.

— James Michener

Geri's Place was a local favorite, a popular 1950s-style diner on Route 44 in Canton, 14 miles west of Hartford. It didn't look like much from the outside, with faded yellow paint peeling from its weathered wooden clapboards. Fronted by a bumpy parking lot and flanked by a couple of small, worn buildings, you might have missed it if you weren't looking for it. But most of Geri Steponitis' customers were regulars, and they knew exactly what they were looking for. No artfully arranged garnishes of melon slices and endive, just good coffee and old-fashioned, stick-to-the-ribs food. Pull the steering-wheel handle on the front door, and you were greeted by 1950s memorabilia, sizzling bacon and eggs and happy chatter. If you stopped by on the morning of July 29, 2005, waitress Judy Mihaly was there to welcome you with a smile.

Shortly before 7 o'clock, one of the regulars arrived. He wore a Geri's Place t-shirt, shorts and sandals. His grayish white hair fell from beneath the blue-and-white-striped railroad engineer's cap atop his head. With his ever-present ear-to-ear smile just below the wide, bushy mustache, he strolled in and announced, "I'm ready to work!" as if he were about to start flipping pancakes and washing dishes. By Chip Stotler standards, this was a fairly low-key opener. Certainly not as over the top as when he and his younger brother, Johnny, decided to smile "hello" to an unsuspecting couple in an adjacent car at a traffic light. At precisely the right instant, the Stotler boys turned toward them, revealing their just-inserted-for-a-moment-like-this "Billy Bob teeth," the sight of which propelled the couple from a standing stop to a rubber-burning departure. Chip and Johnny doubled over in laughter.

That's the way it was with Paul "Chip" Stotler, a strapping 5'11", 42-year-old special education teacher, outdoor adventure educator, doting father of five daughters and devoted husband and best friend to his high school sweetheart, Ellen. A friendly grin, a laugh, some more laughs. He lit up the room, made friends and co-conspirators effortlessly, and touched nearly everyone lucky enough to cross paths with him.

He was particularly upbeat the morning of July 29. "I need a big breakfast," he said to waitress Judy as he ordered one of his favorites, a bacon-and-cheddar omelet. He was on his way from his New Hartford home to work, his last day before vacation. Chip and Ellen would be leaving for Vermont the next day, taking the girls (Cassidy, Kelly, MacKenzie, Kiley and Casey, ages three to eight) for a much-anticipated, two-week getaway. Ellen, a vice president and portfolio manager with Ironwood Capital of Avon and Boston, was home and already loading up the family SUV for their next adventure together.

An assistant director at the Gengras Center, a school for special education students on the campus of Saint Joseph College in West Hartford, Chip had worked there for the past five years.

Here's how the school described itself on its web site[1]:

> The Center is a unique, special education program for elementary, middle and high school students with intellectual, developmental, learning disabilities, and related behavioral challenges…Close collaboration between family, school districts, and other service providers is an important component of the Gengras program…we also provide a lab school for the college students of Saint Joseph College.

Here's how one of Chip's colleagues[2] described the school and children who go there:

> Once upon a time in a forest not so far from here, there were several little villages made up of elves. These elves looked like regular people except they were not very noticeable because of their small size. They were kind, helpful elves who lived in small, modest cabins made of twigs and leaves. Even though they were tiny as a group, they were all a little different…

Chip had a knack for working with these elves. There was one student who had missed several consecutive days of school. Concerned, Chip went to his house. The student saw him and ran. Chip followed him into the house, up the stairs, into his bedroom, out the window and onto the roof. They sat together on the roof and talked. Whatever Chip said, it worked. The student returned to school the next day.

> …sometimes elves were not born healthy and ready to grow and learn like the other elves…some of them could not seem to remember the lessons they had been taught just moments before. No one could really understand

---

1. http://ww2.sjc.edu/gengras/
2. Excerpts from "A Fairy Tale," by John Drewry, one of Chip Stotler's Gengras Center colleagues and friends.

why this happened to some of the elves...these elves had to go to a small patch of the forest that was cleared away to be watched each day and to make sure they were safe and to see if they could be helped enough to become a contributing part of their village. Some of the elves who worked with the disabled were special teachers trained to be very patient...to help them learn how to deal with their anger for being different...

"Chip loved kids," said younger brother Johnny, talking about Chip's other-worldly level of patience. "I would get home from work very frustrated. I'd call Chip and tell him about my bad day. He'd say:

'Did anyone spit at you?'

I'd say 'No.'

'Did anyone try to bite you?'

'No.'

'Then you didn't have a bad day.'"

Gengras Center teachers specialize in finding the hidden strengths in their students. "We look for ways to use active learning as much as possible," explained Chip's colleague Mike Gessford, adventure education director and physical education teacher at the Gengras Center. "We try to create a safe environment for kids to take risks, physical and intellectual risks. Hands-on activity works better for them. Trust building and team cohesion is what lets them earn the right to test themselves on the ropes course at the end of the lesson. Being outside helps. Different strengths show up outdoors. It gives the kids a better chance to shine."

That's one reason why Mike and Chip had spent a good part of the previous day, July 28, working on the Gengras Center playground, where some of the outside adventure education took place. Among its features were walls to scale and ropes to climb. "We were making benches out of some of the trees that had fallen on the property," Mike said. "Chip had a chainsaw; he was covered in wood chips. We had a great time. He went inside after that to do an evaluation. It probably didn't occur to him that he was full of sweat and sawdust."

Working with wood was a passion Chip shared with his five daughters. It wasn't unusual for Stotler neighbors to see Chip and the girls in the yard, all wearing tool belts, putting up the bird houses they had made in the workshop above their garage. On special occasions, rather than getting a Hallmark card, friends of the Stotlers might receive an original, handmade birdhouse, carefully numbered with a router.

Birdhouses weren't the only homemade Stotler creation. Just as he had done for the Gengras School students, Chip made sure his children had a great playscape in their backyard. In addition to building the requisite swings and monkey bars, he asked the girls what special features they wanted. They asked for a picnic table and fort, and he built those, too. Taking special orders from the girls was just something Chip did naturally, even when it came to making dinner.

"He always made everything fun," said his mom, Bobbie Stotler, with a laugh. "Chip would make up little dinner menus and the kids would circle what they wanted. Sometimes he'd end up making five different dinners."

Raising five daughters was, of course, very much a team effort. When one of the twins required a three-day hospital stay, Chip stayed by her side day and night. In between hospital visits, Ellen took care of everything on the home front. "She convinced him one day to go out to lunch to get some fresh air," Bobbie said. "He went right back to the hospital, and Ellen went back home to their other girls including the other twin who missed her sister so much."

One very cold winter day when the teachers and their students were inside their school hut, a snow storm blew in from the north…so fast and fierce that…it was too late to send the students home. In the morning, the elf teachers climbed out and stood upon the roof. Just then, a huge, white, snowy figure came sliding toward the school…the elves saw that the barreling snow figure was actually a giant man who had flowing white hair and a white mustache. He wore blue jeans and a thick, plaid flannel shirt and on top of his head was a blue and white striped engineer's hat…With a few strong but gentle scoops of his large hands, the snow around the school was cleared…From that day on, the giant came to the school every day and encouraged the elf children to climb ladders and walk across beams and every one of them did because the giant was there and never let them fall.

Every winter in New England and other frigid places throughout the world, hardy – some would say "crazy" – souls participated in events with names like the Arctic Dip or Penguin Plunge. Their reasons for jumping into icy ponds and lakes varied, from peer pressure to raising money for good causes to simply wanting to experience the bone-chilling, heart-stopping cold. For most, the event would involve a very quick dip followed by a warm towel in front of a roaring bonfire.

The High 5 Adventure Learning Center in Brattleboro, Vermont held its own "Polar Dip" every year in early February. As a frequent attendee of High 5's winter symposium, Chip became a regular participant in the Polar Dip, but perhaps for his own unique reason. According to one High 5 staffer, "It always appeared that he thoroughly enjoyed it," he said, somewhat incredulously. "He would approach the ice hole, often in costume, always smiling, and leap, without hesitation, into the unknown waters below. And as if one jump was not enough, he'd jump again…and again. One would believe that this was simply to win his High 5 Polar Dip pin, but I honestly believe he just thought it was fun."

Sometimes he would tell a joke or make a funny face and the elves would laugh and laugh until their sides hurt. He was very kind to them and very patient…he always told them if they looked hard enough, they could find fun in every situation…The whole school loved their giant friend with the engineer's cap and they all eagerly came to school each day to try their very best…They all loved the giant very much and knew that he loved them.

Chip finished his breakfast at Geri's Place, said good-bye to Judy and Geri, got into his 1998 Subaru Outback and headed off to the Gengras Center. Ellen called Geri's later that morning looking for him, but he was already gone.

CHAPTER 3

A Dirty Business

It was another late night and early morning for David Wilcox, the 70-year-old owner of American Crushing & Recycling (ACR) of Bloomfield, Conn., a northern suburb of Hartford. While most of his peers were enjoying the perks of retirement, Mr. Wilcox was still working long hours. And "Truck Number 8," a Mack RDS688S tri-axle dump truck, which ACR purchased new in 2000, needed work.

He had worked on the truck the previous night, along with his 24-year-old son, Shaun, and several ACR employees. At around 6:30 on the morning of July 29, 2005, he loaded the 20,000-pound truck with about 50,000 pounds of rough fill – reddish-brown dirt and gravel, tree stumps, large concrete chunks from a broken-up foundation – for a delivery to Avon. At a total of 70,000 pounds, or 35 tons, Truck 8 weighed 24 times more than my 2,892-pound Mercury Cougar. Loading that amount onto even the most well-built truck and hauling it up and down the rolling hills of Connecticut to rugged, uneven construction sites takes its toll. Even so, Truck 8 seemed to have more than its fair share of problems. Aurora Husiak, hired by Wilcox in November 2001, drove Truck 8 for about two-and-a-half years and more than 100,000 miles.

"The truck had front-end problems that would make it difficult to maintain on the road, the truck would move from side to side in the lane and required that I concentrate...to keep it on the road," she said. "It was very hard to make sharp left and right turns, sometimes having to back up a little to make the turn." When she told Mr. Wilcox about it, he said there was "no problem with Truck 8."[1]

Another former ACR employee, Mark Andrade, was assigned to Truck 16. On his second day of work, May 2, 2005, he found hydraulic oil leaks and brake pads that were worn down to the rivets. The brakes squealed. He reported the problem but nothing was done about it for two weeks. Mr. Andrade checked with an ACR mechanic, who told him that when they do full brake jobs, they only replace the shoes. Mr. Andrade once heard Shaun Wilcox say that the company never changes the brake drums, just the shoes – the classic band-aid fix for the wound in need of stitches.

Lessa Chapdelaine, who also drove Truck 8 in the spring and early summer of 2005, said that whenever she needed work done on a truck, she would try to find someone other than David or Shaun Wilcox. They would get mad, she said, and start yelling and say that there was nothing wrong with the truck.

---

1. Arrest warrant affidavit, CFS#: 0500016324, p. 22, point #34

Not so, according to the people who actually drove the truck each day. In addition to the steering problems, Aurora Husiak also reported that Truck 8 was difficult to stop, especially with a full load. There were times when she had to resort to extreme measures, such as using the supplementary maxi brake, similar to a passenger car's emergency brake. According to John Antoniak, a part-time driver and son of David Wilcox's wife, Donna, the brakes on Truck 8 "sucked."[2]

Documenting problems in pre-trip inspections is required by the Connecticut Department of Transportation; a copy of the inspection is to be kept in the truck. But Mr. Wilcox had his own way of keeping the books, according to Ms. Husiak. If drivers found minor problems during their pre-trip inspections, they were to verbally report them only to Mr. Wilcox. If there was a significant problem, a pre-trip inspection form would be filled out and handed directly to Mr. Wilcox, who kept a pre-inspection book hidden in a separate location. A second copy of the form, with no problems listed, would be kept in the truck.

The problems with Truck 8 were part of a long history Wilcox's companies had with state officials. From October 1997 through September 2005, Wilcox Trucking Inc. and American Crushing & Recycling, LLC had compiled a total of 1,136 violations of the Federal Motor Carrier Safety Regulations, 223 of which were serious enough to have his trucks declared "out of service," which meant that inspectors took the trucks off the road immediately.[3]

Truck 8 had been ordered off the road several times since December 2002 after inspections found safety violations, including problems with its brakes in July 2004 and with its steering in October 2004. Each time, the company certified in writing to state officials that it had repaired the vehicle, according to William Seymour, a spokesman for Connecticut's Department of Motor Vehicles (DMV).[4] In other words, DMV was taking the owner's word.

Running a small business isn't easy. Good help can be hard to find. Government regulation can lead to time-consuming and costly operating procedures. Competition is fierce. There were dozens of construction/trucking companies doing business in the greater Hartford area in 2005. Winning new jobs often requires submitting the lowest bid, which reduces profit margins. In fact, despite the long list of operating violations, one of Wilcox's best customers was the state of Connecticut, which often awards contracts solely on the basis of lowest bid.

---

2. Arrest warrant affidavit, CFS#: 0500016324, p. 29, #46
3. Arrest warrant affidavit, CFS#: 0500016324, p. 20, #5
4. *New York Times*, Aug. 2, 2005, "Fatal Truck Crash Prompts Scrutiny"

According to the *Hartford Courant*, "While state inspectors were citing his trucks for scores of safety violations, David Wilcox's companies were racking up something else from the state: payments totaling hundreds of thousands of dollars. Between 1989 and 2001, the state paid Wilcox Trucking more than $1.6 million in state contracts, mostly for delivering sand for snow plows, and for state road projects in Andover, according to state records. In 2002-03, after Wilcox folded his original firm and started American Crushing & Recycling, LLC, the state Department of Transportation paid the company $94,196 for delivering sand."[5]

Wilcox also hustled for smaller jobs. A big part of his business was redistributing dirt. His company would clear land for construction projects, taking fill from the cleared site to store at his Bloomfield company property. Wilcox would then reload that same material for customers who needed fill. It was hard, dirty work with modest profit margins.

So it's not surprising that some small business owners like Wilcox feel pressure to cut corners when it comes to operating expenses. There are a lot of costs to cover, like rent or mortgages on business property, payroll, advertising, utilities, new equipment, maintenance and insurance.

In fact, in early January 2005, Donna Wilcox, who provided administrative support for ACR, canceled the liability insurance on 12 ACR vehicles, including Truck 8, which resulted in a $39,976 credit to ACR.[6] "We really weren't that busy, and we were trying to save some money," she said.[7] Although Donna Wilcox called Webster Insurance to cancel the insurance, absolutely nothing pertaining to the operation of the company happened without the approval or direction of David Wilcox, according to Yvette Melling, a contract administrator for ACR.[8]

If you canceled your passenger car insurance in January 2005, you could expect a letter from the Department of Motor Vehicles (DMV) reminding you in no uncertain terms that Connecticut law requires liability insurance, and that you had 30 days to verify that you had liability insurance. Thanks to a law passed unanimously by Connecticut's legislature in 1993, insurers were required to notify DMV when an individual's car insurance lapsed or was canceled. DMV missives to Connecticut drivers included the following big, bold, all-caps statement:

CONNECTICUT LAW REQUIRES LIABILITY INSURANCE COVERAGE DURING THE REGISTRATION PERIOD. DMV WILL BE NOTIFIED IF INSURANCE IS CANCELED AND MAY SUSPEND YOUR REGISTRATION PRIVILEGES.[9]

---

5. *Hartford Courant*, October 1, 2005, "State Used Wilcox's Firms," Daniel P. Jones and David Owens

6. Arrest Warrant Affidavit, JD-CR-64a Rev. 10-04, p. 2, 4) B

7. Arrest Warrant Affidavit, CFS#: 0500016324, p. 24, point #37

8. Arrest Warrant Affidavit, CFS#: 0500016324, p. 24, point #37

9. State of Connecticut Department of Motor Vehicles, FB1546

But commercial entities such as ACR were under no such scrutiny. They could cancel their liability insurance, and DMV would NOT be notified. The legislation that passed unanimously in 1993 applied only to individual automobile owners and explicitly excluded commercial insurance, creating a gaping loophole through which David Wilcox drove his entire fleet of 12 dump trucks.

Former Hartford Police Detective LeRoy Pittman has been around the block a few times. One of 13 children, he grew up in the north end of Hartford in the 1940s, dropped out of school and joined the Marines. "It was the best move I ever made," he said. "It gave me the discipline I needed. I loved it."

Well, most of it. He didn't like getting up early. "I'm not a morning person, never was," he said. He also didn't like the fact that he wasn't able to get into the flight training program. He wanted to fly jets.

Nevertheless, not long after completing basic training in Montford Point, North Carolina, he was on his way to the other side of the world to fight in Korea, where he served honorably with the First Marine Air Wing. He returned to Hartford, passed the police exam and was soon "walking the beat" in various Hartford neighborhoods. That routine was interrupted at one point during the mid-1950s. Hartford Police couldn't solve a brutal murder in one of its toughest neighborhoods. Officer Pittman was asked to go undercover to see what he could find. Before long, he got the information needed to crack the notorious case. With his street smarts and growing record of accomplishment, he earned his gold detective's badge in the early 1960s. In his spare time, he developed real estate and went back to school, earning his associate's degree, bachelor's degree and, ultimately, his master's degree in education administration from the University of Massachusetts. And in 1965, he finally learned how to fly. He earned his pilot's license and bought a Cessna Skyhawk.

Tall, square shouldered and soft-spoken, Detective Pittman retained his Marine bearing more than half a century after he first pulled on his combat boots. He also retained his dislike of getting up early.

So he surprised himself the last week of July 2005 when he agreed to get up at 5 a.m. to give a virtual stranger a ride to his new job driving trucks in Bloomfield, Conn. Abdulraheem Naafi, a newcomer to Hartford, had recently started renting a room on Sigourney Street from Det. Pittman's friend, Prenzina Holloway. "Getting up early, I just don't do that," Det. Pittman said. "But Raheem was trying to get his life back together. He was very sincere. I've been very lucky in my life. I don't know, I just wanted to help him."

Raheem, 41 years old, needed help. He had a criminal record, which included a robbery conviction, writing a bad check, third-degree assault, sixth-degree larceny and interfering with a police officer. He was from Philadelphia, where he was known as Terrance R. Stokes. It's not clear why he arrived in Hartford early in the summer of 2005. Raheem had spent time at homeless shelters in Stamford, Bridgeport and Hartford.

It's also not clear when he changed his name and embraced the Muslim faith. "Abdulraheem" means "Servant of the Most Compassionate."[10] According to Mrs. Holloway, his new Hartford landlord, he was serious about learning his new faith. "He was trying to change his life," she said. "I never saw him drink or smoke. He'd go to work, come home, sit on the porch, go to bed and get up early and go to work. He didn't want a TV in his room. He would read."

During the last part of July, when he wasn't working, reading or sleeping, Raheem would socialize on the front porch of the Sigourney Street house with Mrs. Holloway and Det. Pittman. "He was such a nice guy," Mrs. Holloway said. "He loved to talk with you. He'd have you laughing. He told me, 'You're my mother here in Hartford.' He called me 'Momma.'"

He was saving money to buy a car. "He said it cost about $600. He wanted to get on his feet again," Det. Pittman said. "He really wanted to drive trucks. That's all he talked about. He liked driving trucks."

David Wilcox's track record eventually caught up with him, or so it appeared. In a March 2000 compliance review by Connecticut's Department of Motor Vehicle Commercial Safety Unit, Wilcox Trucking received a safety rating of unsatisfactory, effectively putting it out of business in April. Undeterred, David Wilcox simply organized American Crushing & Recycling, LLC. As a limited liability corporation, its owners were shielded from liability that could arise as a result of business operations. ACR began doing business in May – at the same address and phone number as Wilcox Trucking, and with the same equipment and procedures. ACR did, however, add a few new vehicles, including Truck 8.

But even though it was new, it wasn't long before problems arose. And Aurora Husiak wasn't the only ACR driver who complained about Truck 8. Wilcox hired Rafael Santiago in March 2005. He said there were problems with Truck 8's brakes the entire time he drove it. Santiago documented these problems a few times a week. At least twice he was almost involved in accidents, he said, due to the brakes not working properly. The truck also had transmission problems – it was difficult to shift into gear. After several months at ACR, Santiago had had enough. He quit.

Just down the road from ACR in Bloomfield, one of its competitors, Lyons Trucking, was also having problems. Large trucks have heavy-duty transmissions with complicated gear ranges. According to owner Nevelle

---

10. http://www.islamicity.com

Lyons, a new driver didn't know how to shift properly and had ruined the transmission on one of his trucks. That new driver was Abdulraheem Naafi. With the truck now sidelined until it could be fixed, there was no vehicle for Raheem to use. Lyons let him go on July 26.

So Raheem was looking for a new job. He didn't have to look far. About a mile away from Lyons Trucking, American Crushing & Recycling was looking for a new driver. David Wilcox hired Raheem on Wednesday, July 27, the day after he was fired from Lyons Trucking. All newly hired drivers are required to pass driving and drug tests before operating a vehicle on their own. Wilcox said Raheem passed the driving test, and that he was scheduled to take a drug test at Concertina, a local drug-testing laboratory, on the afternoon of July 29. According to Concertina, customers are served on a walk-in basis. There are no scheduled appointments.

Whether a test was scheduled or not, Raheem had not yet taken the required test. Nevertheless, Wilcox put Raheem behind the wheel of one of his trucks on July 28, and had him deliver fill to a building lot on top of Avon Mountain where a new house was being built. He made more than a dozen back-and-forth trips that day.[11]

Later that night, Wilcox and his son Shaun, along with several other ACR employees, worked late on repairs. Wilcox was back to work early the following morning. By 6:30 a.m., most of his trucks were already on the road. But Truck 8 remained, which he planned to assign to his new driver, Abdulraheem Naafi, who was late for work.

---

11. Note from author's records: Atty. Ray Hassett said at the June 24, 2009 sentencing of David Wilcox that Naafi had made 20 trips to the Deerfield Road building lot the day before the crash.

CHAPTER 4

Fellow Travelers

By around 7 a.m., the massive morning migration of Farmington Valley residents toward Hartford was beginning. It was a diverse group, from CEOs to summer interns, long-time residents to new citizens from as far away as Belarus, driving the latest-model BMWs or riding as passengers in buses and van pools. Among those tens of thousands of commuters were two middle-aged women with some uncanny similarities.

Office workers Maureen Edlund and Barbara Bongiovanni didn't know each other, but they shared a similar defining moment in their lives. They had both lost their husbands to heart problems 14 years before, leaving each of them suddenly alone to raise a nine-year-old child. They had devoted themselves to supporting Tara Edlund and Vincent Bongiovanni, both of whom were now 22 years old.

In addition to being there for their children, Maureen and Barbara cared for elderly mothers. But even with all those responsibilities, they were approaching a good time in their lives. Their children were doing well, they were loved and respected by family, friends and colleagues, and they were beginning to look forward to life beyond the daily demands of commuting to work and putting in 40 to 60 hours each week.

The Scenic Route

Maureen Edlund was an artist. It wasn't what she was paid for but it was her passion. Her specialty was tole painting, the art of decorative rendering of designs like flowers and beautiful landscapes onto tin and wooden objects such as utensils and furniture. She would look for inspiration wherever she could find it in her busy life. One of those places was Nod Road, which wends its way beside the Farmington River from Avon to Simsbury. That was part of the route she would take each workday morning to her job at Jacobs Vehicle Systems in Bloomfield, even though it would have been a little faster to turn left off Route 44 onto the more well-traveled – and straighter – Hopmeadow Street/Route 10. Instead, she would drive about another mile to the base of Avon Mountain before turning left onto scenic and winding Nod Road.

"This was her morning route because the farms and fields and streams along that road were so beautiful in the morning and it made her think of her tole painting," said Tara, who rode with her mom the previous few summers. Tara was a recent graduate of Hobart College in Geneva, N.Y. Her mom helped get her a summer job at Jacobs, whose property abuts, among other businesses, American Crushing & Recycling, the company owned by David Wilcox. Maureen's destination the morning of July 29 was just a few hundred yards from where David Wilcox stood waiting for his late-for-work driver, Abdulraheem Naafi.

In fact, Wilcox's Mack dump trucks, including Truck 8, had a key safety part that was manufactured in his corporate neighbor's factory, within about a hundred feet of Maureen's desk. "As the maker of the world famous *Jake Brake*® engine retarders, Jacobs Vehicle Systems is recognized as the industry leader in developing and manufacturing commercial vehicle retarding systems that help large trucks slow down more easily. With more than 40 years experience in the business, Jacobs is known for its innovative business practices, modern manufacturing methods and a level of research and development investment rivaled only by the aerospace industry."[1]

On the market for nearly 50 years, the *Jake Brake* was invented by Clessie L. Cummins who once tried to set a new truck speed record across the U.S. continent along with two other drivers, one of whom warned Cummins about a dangerous downgrade west of Barstow, Calif. That warning "failed to register when the sign for Cajun Pass appeared. Soon, however, I realized my error," Cummins wrote. "The brakes wouldn't hold. Now running in third gear, I tried desperately to get into a lower speed. Nothing down, I saw I would just have to ride it out. I suddenly saw something moving across the road ahead. I realized with new alarm that a freight train was cutting across our path. As we raced inexorably toward the crossing and doom, the train's caboose loomed out of the darkness. Its red lights cleared the highway just as we reached the tracks. We had escaped certain death by inches."[2]

That terrifying experience inspired Mr. Cummins to invent the *Jake Brake*, which – when used correctly – helps slow large vehicles on steep downhill grades by turning the engine into a giant air compressor, thus "retarding" its power and slowing the vehicle considerably, making it easier to stop with regular brakes. Anyone who has driven near a decelerating truck would probably recognize the loud, staccato growl of the *Jake Brake* at work.

Tara's father, Dave, worked for Jacobs. Shortly after he died, the company offered Maureen a job, where she worked for 13 years. "It's a very family-oriented company," Tara said. "The leadership had given me some money towards college and also instituted an award in my dad's name: 'The Dave Edlund Quality Award,' which is still handed out to this day."

1. http://www.jakebrake.com/about-us/
2. http://www.jakebrake.com/about-us/history.php

Before meeting her future husband, Maureen – or "Moe" as she was called by those who knew her well – taught elementary school in Lompoc, Calif. and Enfield, Conn. After meeting and marrying, the couple and Dave's two children from his first marriage, Peter and Kristan, settled in Grand Blanc, Mich., where Jacobs had transferred Dave to take on a regional sales manager job. Tara was born in 1982, and within a few years Peter joined the Navy and Kristan was off to college. "I grew up very much as an only child," Tara said. "My mother loved being a stay-at-home mom. She often referred to her years in Michigan as the best years of her life."

In 1989, Dave was transferred back to Connecticut and the Edlund family settled into a new home in Canton. Less than two years later, Dave died suddenly. "His heart just stopped beating," said Tara, who was then nine years old. About a year earlier, he had been diagnosed with Type II diabetes and high cholesterol. "He attacked both problems with vigor and enthusiasm," Tara said. "My mom found and invented low-cholesterol, low-fat meals, and my dad was vigilant about checking his blood sugar. He had been given a clean bill of health about a month before he died."

Shortly after Dave's death, Jacobs offered Maureen the job as a warranty administrator. She eventually transferred to the human resources department as the company receptionist. After Tara left for college, Maureen began working three nights and Sundays at Wal-Mart in Avon to help pay for Tara's education. On Saturdays, Maureen took care of her elderly mother, Margaret.

"My mom never faltered in her support of me and my ambitions throughout high school," Tara said. "She encouraged me to go on a Canton exchange program trip to Russia. And when it came time to choose a college, she encouraged me to choose the best fit first, saying that we would worry about the price after."

Maureen was proud of her daughter, and she wanted her to have all the opportunities she may have missed herself during her childhood in Springfield, Mass., everything from Girl Scouts to Irish dance lessons to attending the college of her choice. "She worked very hard, and Tara was her focal point," said Bobbie-Ann Marquis, former owner of Maggie Dailey's Fine Celtic Wares on Route 44 in Canton. As it turns out, Maureen was Ms. Marquis' very first customer. "When I opened my store, Maureen was the first person to walk in the door. She was very connected to her Irish heritage, and wanted to work there."

In addition to selling authentic, finely crafted items imported from Ireland, Scotland, England and Wales, Bobbie wanted Maggie's to be a "healing place," a cultural center with live music, classes on Irish history and Irish dance lessons. "I'll always remember this one St. Patrick's Day," Ms. Marquis said. "Tara was doing a beautiful Irish reel, a lively dance. She was so light on her feet, so young and graceful. I can still see the love and pride on Maureen's face as she watched her daughter."

Of course, Maureen had her own artistic calling, and painting became her escape from the heavy demands on her time. "Maureen was a phenomenal artist," said Elissa Kiessling, R.N., manager of Medical Services at Jacobs, who attended several painting classes with Maureen. "I was obviously a beginner, but Maureen was very accomplished. She was a perfectionist. If she didn't like it, she would do it over and over again to get it just right. She did some beautiful winter scenes and flowers, the most magnificent flowers."

Maureen's perfectionism was also evident in her work at Jacobs, where she was a popular and highly regarded employee. On rare occasions, due to her heavy workload, Maureen would end up running a few minutes late in the morning. "Several days a week, Maureen would start work at 8 a.m. and go all the way to 10 at night at her other job," Ms. Kiessling said. So no one paid much attention on the morning of July 29, 2005, when Maureen was not at her desk at the start of the work day. But as a few minutes grew into many, which was very unusual, her colleagues took notice. "She had a cell phone that she would use for emergencies," Ms. Kiessling said. "But we didn't hear from her. We were getting very worried."

"Nobody's Going to Remember Me"

While Maureen Edlund was running late, Barbara Bongiovanni, 54 years old, was on the road earlier than usual. "She normally came in later on Fridays," said Susan Dalgleish, Barbara's colleague in the business department of Saint Francis Hospital in Hartford. "But she had a doctor's appointment later in the day, so she wanted to put in some extra time earlier to make up for the time she would be away."

Taking care of her responsibilities, Barbara Bongiovanni, or "Bongi," as she was affectionately called by her long-time colleagues, would never leave anything unfinished for coworkers to handle. They had been through a lot together, including the heart attack that killed Barbara's husband 14 years earlier.

"We had a special bond with her because of that tragedy, when she lost her husband," said Della Copeland, who had starting working with Barbara more than 20 years ago. "He was such a nice person, a sweet guy."

So the full responsibility of raising her son, Vincent, who was nine years old when his father died, fell to Barbara. It wasn't easy. The two of them lived in a large raised ranch, a few miles east of the tight-knit Italian neighborhood in Torrington where Barbara grew up. In the decade between losing his dad and finding Jesus, Vincent put himself and his mom through a little bit of hell. "I was a bad kid," he readily admitted. "I'm not proud of that. Mom did the best she could."

Vincent was raised a Catholic and regularly attended catechism classes.

After his father died and as he approached his teenage years, Vincent was drawn to drugs and alcohol. "Mom would give and give and give," Vincent said. "But I turned my back on God, and sinned all I could."

Exasperated, Barbara resorted to "tough love." "She reached the end of the road with me," Vincent said. "She kicked me out of the house in 2001. It was the best thing for me." But the turnaround didn't come right away. "I was on the street, living in caves, it was tough," he said. "I was high on drugs and ended up getting convicted of robbery. Mom came to see me in jail all the time. She helped me. There was that bulletproof glass wall between us. She prayed for me."

While incarcerated, Vincent went to every church service he could, no matter the denomination. "I read the Bible and prayed," he said. "I came to God on my knees. I was in jail only two years; it could have been seven. Mom took me back. She took care of me. She saw how God turned me around."

Her own childhood on East Main Street near downtown Torrington, a small working-class city just beyond the Litchfield hills in northwestern Connecticut, could not have been more different.

"We lived above our uncle's bake shop," said Floyd Amicone, Barbara's older brother. "On the same street, our father owned a diner and our aunts ran a dress shop. We would get fresh, hot donuts right from my uncle's oven after we did chores for him, like folding bakery boxes."

Eventually, the Amicone family moved to the rural town of Harwinton, a few miles southeast of Torrington. Pretty and popular, Barbara had her share of friends. After finishing high school, she met Carmen Bongiovanni, who worked for the post office. They married, had a son, Vincent, and enjoyed their lives together until Carmine suddenly died.

"It was devastating," said Barbara's colleague Della Copeland. "It brought us all a little closer."

The ladies of Saint Francis Hospital's business department grew into their own little family, sharing hopes, dreams, joys and tragedies. They also shared an unpleasant-tasting health drink called noni juice, made from a fruit grown in the Asia-Pacific region. "It was supposed to be good for you, but it looked like dirt and tasted like dirt," Susan Dalgleish said with a laugh. "One minute Bongi was into fitness, and next she'd bring in those cannolis."

Giving was just something Barbara did. "There was no reason, she would just give," said Michelle Saunders. "She'd come in to the office with a box of whatever. 'Anybody want this?' She brought in anything she thought you could use."

Barbara had more than the usual to give away in the first half of 2005. She was engaged to Ted Connole, and they were talking about retiring and moving to Virginia. That may have been one of her reasons for downsizing from her raised ranch, and moving back to downtown Torrington and into a small apartment. "She had recently sold her house, and found a new apartment on Prospect Street," said her brother, Floyd. "She was very happy about that. She really loved it. She liked to get home from work and relax or take a walk."

Despite the love and respect she had earned from family, friends and colleagues, Barbara apparently didn't believe she had made much of an impression. "No one's going to remember me," Barbara told her Saint Francis colleagues as she contemplated retirement. Before she left work each day, she would carefully clean her desk, leaving nothing out of order. "I'd say to her, 'Bongi, why do you always clean up your desk?'" Michelle said. "She'd say, 'So if I don't come back, then I don't have to worry about it.'"

On the evening of July 28, Barbara visited her son in his new apartment near the Naugatuck River in Torrington. "She asked if I wanted to go to dinner with her," Vincent said. "I told her no, 'the flesh will die.' It's more important to pray together and read the Bible. We read the Book of Luke. She gave me a big hug and kiss. I told her I loved her. She said, 'Good-bye for now, I'll see you soon.'"

CHAPTER 5

Last Chances

Abdulraheem Naafi was running out of chances. He was determined to put his difficult past behind him and make good at his new start in Hartford and on his new job driving trucks. Despite his determination and optimism, he may have had an inkling that the odds were lining up against him.

"I'm going to work for the bad guys," he told Prenzina Holloway, his Hartford landlord, just before starting his new job with American Crushing & Recycling after he was fired by Lyons Trucking. "Mr. Wilcox said he'd give me a job."

But there was trouble almost immediately. "He told Wilcox that the truck needed to be fixed," said Mrs. Holloway. "He told us the truck didn't have any brakes." With his history of troubles, however, Raheem desperately wanted to succeed at his new job. He was reluctant to make waves.

LeRoy Pittman, the former Marine and Hartford Police detective, had dinner with Raheem on July 28. "He was so thrilled about getting this new job, that's all he talked about," Mr. Pittman said. "But he told me that one of the guys at work told him, 'You know about the brakes on your truck, right?' Raheem told me he went to a mechanic and mentioned the brakes. And the mechanic just sort of blew him off."

After dinner that night, Raheem returned to his room on Sigourney Street in Hartford. "We were on the porch," Mrs. Holloway remembered. "He said, 'Momma, I'm so tired.' That boy went to his room, took a bath, and went to bed."

The next morning, Friday, July 29, Mr. Pittman once again got up early to drive Raheem to work. "We were running a little late," Mr. Pittman said. "When we pulled into the yard, it was about 6:35. I know because I looked at my watch. As we pulled in, Raheem pointed out his boss, Mr. Wilcox, who was standing in the door. I told him if he had anything to say, blame it on me. I was the driver. There was only one dump truck left in the yard when Raheem got out of the car. There were no other trucks. Raheem got out of the car, and I left."

That one truck was Truck 8. Mr. Wilcox loaded it with about 50,000 pounds of reddish-brown dirt, gravel, boulders, tree stumps and large slabs of a broken-up concrete foundation. Truck drivers are supposed to inspect their vehicles carefully each day before driving. Many do not. Given that he was late, that he was a new driver with a checkered past, and that Mr.

Wilcox had a reputation for yelling at drivers who complained about the condition of their trucks, it's unlikely that Raheem circled Truck 8 that morning and carefully inspected it.

He got behind the wheel just before 7 o'clock, as morning rush-hour traffic was reaching its peak, and drove toward Avon.

"We don't make trucks. We build legends."

That's what the Mack Truck marketing literature says. "The track record is indisputable. The very first Mack ever built in 1900 ran for over a million miles. Another model with amazing tenacity and traction helped the Allies win World War I. Throughout the twentieth century, America has been building at a furious rate. And at the center of it all is Mack. The construction industry relies on Mack trucks to handle the most challenging jobs. After all, our machines are legendary. They last for decades. They have amazing reliability. They are synonymous with tough, strong and powerful."[1]

But Mack's "amazing reliability" requires good maintenance, considering the beating the trucks endure carrying massive loads to rugged construction sites. When Raheem climbed high up into the cab of Truck 8 on the sunny summer morning of July 29, 2005, he may have only suspected it was in bad shape. If he had inspected Truck 8 that morning, he may very well have found some problems. But it's highly unlikely that he would have found all 20 of Truck 8's violations[2] of the Connecticut Vehicle Safety Code, some of which could be detected only with time-consuming diagnostic tools. Four violations were so dangerous – three involving the brakes – that had any one of them been discovered, the vehicle would have been declared "out of service," or too dangerous to drive. In other words, if Truck 8 had been stopped for inspection during its trip to Avon, it would have been taken off the road immediately. Its load would have been transferred to another vehicle, and Truck 8 would have been towed to a garage for repairs.

Under the best of circumstances, it's not easy to control a 20,000-pound, 400-horsepower, 12-wheel, 13-gear, triple-axle dump truck loaded with 50,000 pounds of rough fill, just short of the maximum legal load. At a total of 70,000 pounds, or 35 tons, Truck 8 was about 20 times heavier than a typical mid-sized car like a Subaru Outback. To control this kind of heavy-duty, unwieldy beast, truck drivers rely on steering, downshifting, brakes and experience. On July 29, 2005, Raheem and Truck 8 may have been short on all four.

---

1. ©2005 Mack Trucks, Inc. 1B-CT-5/05-SWBR/20M
2. Arrest warrant affidavit, CFS#: 0500016324, p. 10, #24.

He had obtained his commercial driver's license in Connecticut on March 26, 1999. It's not clear what practical experience Raheem had driving heavy-duty trucks. But it is clear that he had trouble handling the complicated gear ranges of a truck he drove for Lyons Trucking. According to owner Nevelle Lyons, Raheem ruined the transmission on one of his trucks. The day after being dismissed from Lyons Trucking, Raheem was hired by Mr. Wilcox.

Aurora Husiak, the ACR employee who drove Truck 8 for two-and-a-half years and more than 100,000 miles, said it was difficult to handle, specifically noting that it was hard to make sharp left and right turns. Truck 8's brakes – *all* its brakes, including the regular, maxi and emergency brakes – were either in very bad shape or completely deteriorated. There was also a serious issue with the clutch assembly and transmission. Truck 8's history already included complaints from previous drivers about trouble shifting into the proper gear. The complex clutch system became more challenging due to a faulty clutch plate. When the previous clutch plate was replaced on Truck 8, the pilot bearing apparently was never reinstalled. That caused the clutch plate to wobble, which made it even more difficult to shift.

So Raheem had his hands full as he maneuvered Truck 8 onto Route 44 west and began climbing the West Hartford side of Avon Mountain. Along the way, on his left, he passed the entrance to the exclusive Renbrook School for children in pre-school through grade 9. To his right, as the mountain leveled off for a stretch, he passed the Metropolitan District's Reservoir #6, a popular place to walk and enjoy the woods and water views. A little farther west, near where the Metacomet Trail intersects Route 44, massive new houses were being built in exclusive new developments on both sides of the road.

The grade began to get steeper again as Raheem approached the Avon town line and the crest of the mountain. After crossing into Avon and reaching the highest point, the road began, ever so slightly, its downhill trajectory. A big yellow sign warns drivers of an upcoming 10 percent downgrade, a 10-foot drop in altitude for every 100 feet of road.

"That's a real seriously steep grade," said Phillip Wilson, author of *Driver – Six Weeks in an Eighteen-Wheeler*. "The main thing [a driver should do] is start out slowly and don't go any faster than slowly."[3]

Raheem knew from his many deliveries for ACR the day before that he had to prepare for a sharp left turn onto Deercliff Road, two-tenths of a mile past the town line. Workers were already at his intended destination – the $3.6 million spec house about to be built just down the road at 147 Deercliff, the one with the real estate listing boasting "magnificent western views, extraordinary style and design...a private sanctuary done in grand scale."

---

3. WTIC Radio, interview with Ray Dunaway, Sept. 7, 2007

On this day, July 29, 2005, Raheem missed the turn.

Why didn't he make the very same turn that he had made at least a dozen times the day before? Truck 8's third axle was down to help support the full load, so the turning radius was wider than usual. But he had driven a different truck the day before. Was that truck in better condition? Was Raheem not able to slow Truck 8 enough this morning to make that sharp left turn? Did he think he could simply turn around at the next available intersection? He was new to the Hartford area, and likely had never traveled any farther west than Deercliff Road. He probably did not have any idea what was around the corner from Deercliff Road when he missed his turn.

Eric Strangefeld was driving in the same direction that morning. Just past the crest of the mountain, he saw Raheem going very slowly and struggling with the truck in the right lane as he passed him on the left. He said the truck's brake lights were going on and off. "And I heard the sound of air brakes going on and off," Mr. Strangefeld said. "Something was wrong."

CHAPTER 6

Diverse Paths to Harm's Way

Chip Stotler, Maureen Edlund, Barbara Bongiovanni and I had plenty of company on the morning of July 29, 2005, as we drove our cars through Canton toward Avon. Thousands of people made that eastward trip every weekday morning to their jobs on the other side of the mountain. Most Farmington Valley commuters drive toward Route 44, coming from as far west as the small, river mill and factory cities of Torrington and Winsted, and from the rural back roads of New Hartford, Barkhamsted, Canton and Simsbury.

It was a relentless flow, gathering more and more volume from all the traffic tributaries along the way. That flow was interrupted intermittently by a series of traffic lights. The last major stop on the Avon side of the mountain was at its base, just past the bridge over the Farmington River, at the intersection of Routes 44 and 10, and Nod Road. To the north were the Blue Fox Run and Tower Ridge golf courses. To the south were Nassau's Furniture Store and the Avon Cider Mill. On the corner, just past the light, on either side of Route 44, were Avon Old Farms Inn and Avon Old Farms Hotel. Looming directly ahead was Avon Mountain.

Every 65 seconds, just as two or three cars typically accelerate to escape through the yellow, the light at the base of Avon Mountain turns red, stopping at least a dozen or so vehicles in four eastbound lanes.

Mountain of Reputation

Tammy and Michael Cummings were in the market for a new house in the spring of 2005. They liked a house they saw in New Hartford, 17 miles west of Hartford. They liked the look of it, a colonial in a new development of 68 colonials, capes and raised ranches. They liked its size – plenty of room for the two of them and their little Pomeranian, Chewbacca. They liked the backyard, adjacent to 14 acres of state forest. They liked the garage, and the open floor dining room and kitchen area. In fact, there was only one thing they didn't like: the mountain between the house and Saint Francis Hospital in Hartford, where Michael worked as an information technology supervisor.

"I didn't want to drive Avon Mountain every day; it had a reputation," Michael said, citing the history of accidents. He wanted to find a new home farther north, in Simsbury or Granby. That way he could take a more northerly route into Hartford, avoiding Avon Mountain. But for the type of home they wanted, Simsbury and Granby would put more of a strain on the young couple's budget than they were willing to take on at this time in their lives. They moved into the New Hartford house on June 1, 2005.

Michael's concern about Avon Mountain was well founded. From 2002 through 2005, there were 290 reported accidents on the 3.1-mile stretch of Route 44 that traverses Avon Mountain,[1] not including at least six times when trucks lost their brakes and barreled down the Avon side of the mountain and through the busy intersection at its base. Miraculously, no one was seriously injured. Even with its well-documented history, little had been done to make the road safer. Among state and local government officials, there had been lots and lots and lots of talk, but precious little action. In the Dec. 16, 1998 edition of *The Hartford Courant*, Avon Mountain Road resident Don Havens said the proposed modifications for Route 44 traffic flow and safety were "fine, fine, fine." His concern was "getting these changes made – fast!"[2] He was right to be concerned. Despite the high number of crashes, the road-improvement plans on the drawing board in the 1990s were still only in the talking stage in the spring of 2005.

On July 29, 2005, when Michael was about to leave for work, the sight of new lawn equipment he had purchased the day before in the back of his 2002 Dodge Caravan triggered a memory of a car accident. About six years ago, one of his friends hit a tree. A surfboard in the back of his car shot forward and struck him in the head. So Michael took a few extra minutes to remove the lawn mower and weed whacker before starting his trip to Hartford.

A few miles down the road from his new house, Michael realized that he had forgotten his wallet. He went back home to get it. Even with those few delays in his morning routine, Michael was in a good mood. "It was a beautiful day, and it was Friday," he said. "When he came back to get his wallet, I heard him singing to himself," Tammy said.

Michael had one more stop. A new Citgo station with a Dunkin' Donuts had opened one week earlier, a few hundred yards from the base of Avon Mountain. He stopped to buy a cup of coffee.

Meanwhile, Tammy was beginning her trip to work at the mechanical engineering firm of Macri Associates in Simsbury. Every day, as part of her morning ritual, she would say a prayer for Michael and herself to arrive safely at work. She had just finished the prayer when she received an unexpected call on her cell phone.

---

1. Capitol Region Council of Governments, "Automated Speed Enforcement on Avon Mountain," Tom Maziarz, director of Transportation Planning
2. *Hartford Courant*, Dec. 16, 1998, "Route 44 Corridor Discussed"

Five-Minute Head Start

Walk to the top of the hill in Center Cemetery in Simsbury, established in 1688, and you'll see a commanding view of the Metacomet Ridge and the valley. If you take that walk any weekday morning at around 7 o'clock, you might also see Dr. Scott Kurtzman, who lived nearby, and his German Shepherd, Misha, walking among the gravestones of the Phelps, Eno and Ellsworth families, in addition to the hundreds of other grave markers of Simsbury residents at their final earthly resting place.

Noah Phelps is the most celebrated Revolutionary War hero from Simsbury, "as it was his spying which led to the capture of Fort Ticonderoga by Ethan Allen and his Green Mountain Boys."[3] A crypt inside the Eno family mausoleum notes that William Phelps Eno, who lived from June 3, 1858 to December 3, 1945, was a "Highway Traffic Control Pioneer." A plaque on the cemetery's "Memorial Gateway," donated by Lemuel Stoughton Ellsworth and his wife, Jane Toy Ellsworth, in 1922, reads:

ERECTED TO THE MEMORY AND HONOR
OF THOSE CITIZENS OF SIMSBURY WHO
STEADFAST IN THEIR CONCEPTION OF RIGHT
FAITHFUL IN THEIR PERFORMANCE OF DUTY
AND UNSELFISH IN THEIR DEVOTION TO COUNTRY
SERVED THE CAUSE OF JUSTICE AND HUMANITY
IN THE WORLD WAR 1914-1918[4]

Duty, being unselfish, doing the right thing – these were expectations Scott Kurtzman grew up with. "I was taught that we have an obligation to help others," he said, remembering the lessons he learned from his parents, from his Jewish faith, and from his participation in the Boy Scouts' Order of the Arrow, which focuses on community service.

Taking care of people became his life's work. In the spring of 2005, the 50-year-old father of three was named director of surgery at Waterbury Hospital. But he still kept his hand in one of his other passions, teaching. And on the morning of July 29, instead of heading west toward Waterbury, Dr. Kurtzman turned his 2000 Lexus SUV east toward the University of Connecticut Health Center in Farmington. He was scheduled to lead an 8 o'clock workshop on breast-cancer detection with third-year medical students.

Thanks to Misha, he was getting an early start that morning. "She did her business faster than usual," he said, "so I was on the road about five minutes earlier."

---

3. "The Society of Colonial Wars in the State of Connecticut,"
   www.colonialwarsct.org/simsbury.htm
4. "The Society of Colonial Wars in the State of Connecticut,"
   www.colonialwarsct.org/simsbury.htm

A Job To Do

Frank Juan, a 65-year-old bus driver for E. J. Kelley Co., did something on the morning of July 29, 2005, that he did about once a decade – he called in sick. In his 40-plus years of driving buses, he had missed maybe five days of work. And his wife Ann had a premonition. She didn't want him to go to work.

But Kelley Transit was short of drivers this morning, so Frank pulled himself together and did what he always did – he got up to get the job done. Frank Juan, with his compact frame, short dark-gray hair and boisterous personality, was nothing if not rock-solid loyal and dependable.

Ramona, his fiercely devoted daughter, knew that about her father. And she had an important job for him, too, a job only he could do. As she dreamed of her rapidly approaching, September 10 wedding day, she knew her dad had to be right there with her, to walk her down the aisle, just as she had always known he would. "He had to be there," she said, with a knowing intensity. "No one else could walk me down that aisle."

But first things first. Frank made his way to the bus yard in Torrington, climbed the three steps into the driver's seat of Kelley Transit Bus 200 and, at around 6:30 a.m., headed out to his first stop. His 16-year-old granddaughter, Alicia, was planning to go to work with him. When she did, she sat right up front near her grandfather. But something came up at the last minute, and Alicia couldn't make the trip with him.

One by one, Frank's passengers stepped onto Bus 200, including several of his regulars –Doug Smith, father of five boys (ages 6-13), a director at The Travelers in Hartford, and wrestling coach at Winsted High School; and Debbie Della Valle who worked at The Hartford.

"I usually take the earlier bus," Doug said. "But I woke up a few minutes late and decided to eat breakfast and take my time. It was kind of a fluke that I was on the later bus."

"Frank was smiling; he was in good spirits," said Debbie. "He's a typical guy, busting you for everything. If you were wearing a skirt, he'd say, "Nice legs." But we'd give it right back to him, like harassing him when we smelled cigarette smoke. He was trying to quit."

That Frank was no angel was part of his gruff charm. One of his colleagues recalled how Frank would never change the destination sign just above the windshield of his bus. "Each driver is supposed to change it for the next guy," the colleague recalled with a laugh. "I'd say, 'Hey, Frankie, you forgot to change the sign again.' He'd just growl and wave his hand with the cigarette as he walked away."

On July 29, 2005, by the time Frank guided Bus 200 through Winsted, Barkhamsted, New Hartford, Canton and into Avon, he had only eight passengers, instead of the usual 15 to 20. But it was a beautiful Friday morning in the middle of summer. It was a good day to be on vacation.

In His Blood

Megan Cheshire had a pretty good idea of what she was getting herself into when she married Todd Myers in October 2004. By that date, the then 27-year-old West Hartford police officer, a graduate of Simsbury High School and Marist College, was already a six-year veteran of the department. Law enforcement was in his blood, an integral part of his everyday life. "I grew up with it," he said. His dad, Ken, served in the Simsbury Police Department for 30 years, and was also a member of the Simsbury Volunteer Fire Department, as was Todd.

Shortly after they had met in 1999, Megan organized a big party for mutual friends. "Todd was going to pick up some things for the party and then help me set up," she said. "Time went by and people were arriving, but he wasn't there." Turns out he was literally hanging off the side of a ridge on Talcottt Mountain Ridge rescuing a hang glider.

"Megan is very patient," Todd said. "She's a saint." Standing 5' 10" and a muscular 220 pounds, with a crew cut and energetic demeanor, Todd looks like a middle linebacker, an appearance that doesn't hurt when someone needs to take charge of a chaotic situation.

Certain habits that might seem odd to a "civilian" – someone not involved with law enforcement, fire fighting and emergency medical services – don't even raise an eyebrow with the initiated. Like when Todd leaves for work in the morning and grabs his wallet, keys and six-inch, jet-black, razor-sharp, Benchmade® utility knife. "I carry it with me all the time," he said.

It was with him the morning of July 29, 2005. Wearing a white t-shirt tucked into his dark blue uniform slacks, he got into his 2004 Dodge pickup truck and started his regular morning commute to the West Hartford Police Station. He checked his voicemail while still in his driveway, which took about 30 seconds. Then he took off and, within a few minutes, was on Route 44 and driving east toward Avon Mountain.

"It was a typical Friday morning," he remembered. "It was a sunny day. I had the air conditioner and radio on. It was about 7:30."

The Rookie and the Reverend

At 23 years old, Jason Reid was the newest and youngest member of the Avon Police Department. By July 29, 2005, he had been patrolling Avon roads for two months. His most memorable incident thus far had been a foot chase with a shoplifter. But on this day, his main focus was road safety. And he had company. Riding with him was the oldest member of the department, the Rev. Jon Widing, its 68-year-old chaplain.

"I'd been chaplain for about 10 years; I'm an old hand," he said. "My practice is generally to ride one day a week for an hour or two so I can be with the officers on the road. I usually do that on Friday mornings."

In today's politically charged atmosphere, one wonders if the existence of the position of chaplain could be considered a violation of church and state. And why is a chaplain needed anyway? "The simple answer is they don't need me. I'm not necessary in any urgent, practical sense," wrote Kate Braestrup, chaplain for the Maine Warden Service and author of *Here If You Need Me*, a true story about her experiences. "But I'm told that it is helpful to have a chaplain present at a search or an accident, that by taking on the task of being with the victim's family, I free the wardens for other tasks. Perhaps more important, as a minister (as opposed to some other brand of helping professional), I serve as a symbol of a profound truth. My uniformed presence signifies a human and humane understanding on the part of wardens and the wider community that the body in the woods or in the water is not just a practical problem, but a matter of tremendous spiritual significance for those most intimately involved. As reverend, I can express our reverence."[5]

Rev. Widing knows firsthand about the importance of being there, of being present at emotionally wrenching events, such as those of September 11, 2001. "I served as a chaplain during 9/11 in New York," he said. "I was at Ground Zero. When it became a recovery operation, I went to the morgue for nine months as a chaplain as they brought bodies in. I would be there and talk with the rescue workers."

As much as he understood the importance of being there for them, Rev. Widing itched to be more involved. "I've always wanted to be more hands-on," he said. "I've been told for years that I was too old."

On the morning of July 29, 2005, advanced age was not an issue for the rookie officer, Jason Reid. "I was brand new," he said. "I got my keys, checked my car and was out the door and on the road by 7:05. I just grabbed my stuff and left, no coffee with the guys or anything. Rev. Widing got in the car with me, and we took off on patrol."

It wasn't long before Officer Reid had his first stop of the day, a speeding car on Arch Road. "It was a doctor from Avon," he said. "She was going to an appointment in Hartford, going 58 miles per hour." The speed limit was 30. "Just as I was handing her the ticket, a call came in."

It was the police dispatcher. Even though he was new, Officer Reid could read between the lines. "I could tell by the tone of her voice that it was bad," he said. "You can tell if it's a routine call. They talk slowly. If it's not routine, they talk faster. She was talking really fast."

---

5. *Here If You Need Me*, by Kate Braestrup; Little, Brown and Company; Hachette Book Group USA; p. 103

A New Life

Dr. Elena Tomasi had come a long way before landing her new job as a dentist with the Aspen Dental Group – seven time zones, 4,300 miles and one vast ocean, to be exact. Five years earlier, she was practicing her profession in Minsk, the capital of Belarus, the eastern European country that declared its independence from the Soviet Union in 1991.

As a little girl growing up in the small town of Shereshevo, Dr. Tomasi fondly recalls bicycling across the nearby border with Poland, about an hour away, to spend time with a friend. She remembers seeing religious statues and pictures of saints and angels in her friend's home. "The practice of religion was discouraged in the Soviet Union," she said. "You didn't want to get in trouble with the government. As I was growing up, I always felt that something was missing in my life."

Although she did well in her native country, life in Belarus was not easy. According to *The Economist*, a London-based news magazine, Belarus ranked 100 of the 111 countries listed in its 2005 "Worldwide Quality of Life Index," which measures factors such as income, health, freedom, unemployment, family life, climate, political stability and security, gender equality, and family and community life.[6] And the country continues to suffer from nuclear fallout from the 1986 Chernobyl disaster, which took place in neighboring Ukraine.

So when Orlando Tomasi of Torrington, Conn., proposed to her, she accepted and moved to the U.S. in 2000. Although she had received rigorous dental training in Belarus, she still needed another few years of schooling to get her license to practice in the US. She graduated from the University of Connecticut in early 2005, and started working in Aspen's Glastonbury office on July 11, 2005.

"I was very excited," Dr. Tomasi said. "I felt like life had just begun again." Except for all the traffic lights, even the 55-mile commute from Torrington, over Avon Mountain, through Hartford and into Glastonbury, didn't bother her.

She was running about 10 minutes late on the morning of July 29. Although she normally wore medical scrubs to work, she wanted to look a little nicer on this Friday. "I wanted to dress up a little," Dr. Tomasi said in her nearly flawless English, her second language, which she speaks with a Belarusian accent. She had bought a new outfit at an Ann Taylor clothing boutique the previous day, white pants and a black-and-white shirt. That morning, she spent a little extra time doing her hair.

As she approached Avon Mountain, she remembers wanting to pass the Kelley Transit commuter bus. "I usually drive in the right lane. But

---

6. "The world's best country," www.economist.com/media/pdf/
   QUALITY_OF_LIFE.PDF

I was in the left lane that day. I really wanted to pass the bus – you don't want to follow the bus going up the mountain. Sometimes no matter where you are, you can't be a winner. I looked in the side-view mirror, and I saw the bus driver. He was yawning, and I remember his face very well. 'Okay, the guy needs a cup of coffee,' I thought to myself. Finally, right before the traffic light at the foot of Avon Mountain, I passed the bus and got into the right lane."

Just ahead of Elena, Todd Russo was on his way to his job at the Connecticut Audubon Society in Glastonbury. A car was following so close behind that Todd decided to speed up and drive through the yellow light rather than stop and risk getting hit by the tailgater, who also sped through the by-then red light.

The rest of us approaching that red light settled into the available slots in the four westbound lanes at the base of Avon Mountain. Maureen Edlund was first in the far left lane, planning to turn left onto scenic Nod Road. I was directly to her right, first in the left center lane, just a few hundred feet from Avon Old Farms Inn and the banquet room where Chris and I danced our first wedding dance. Directly to my right was Richard Frieder, a librarian at the Hartford Public Library. And to his right, in the far right lane, was Dr. Iris Rich, who was preparing to turn right toward Farmington.

Another two dozen or so vehicles pulled up behind us. Michael Cummings was also right up front, and Barbara Bongiovanni was behind him. Chip Stotler was in the second row in the right center lane. Right behind Chip was Dr. Tomasi and, behind her, in the fourth row, were Frank Juan and the eight passengers on his Kelley Transit bus. Coming up in the far right lane was Dr. Kurtzman. And trailing a little further behind was West Hartford Police Officer Todd Myers.

For those of us up front, our places were set. We were strapped in, locked in, boxed in. There was no place to go. No more jockeying for position. No more lanes to change. No more gas, coffee or breakfast to stop for. No more wallets to retrieve. No more dogs to walk. No more tweaking the twists of fate that brought us to that place at that moment in time. Nothing to do but sit in our idling cars and wait for the light at the intersection, the intersection of Nod Road and Routes 44 and 10, of happenstance and destiny, of wrong place and wrong time.

CHAPTER 7

"So This Is How I'm Going to Die"

There's a train leaving nightly called when all is said and done
Keep me in your heart for awhile

— *Warren Zevon*

Abdulraheem Naafi missed the left turn onto Deercliff Road and headed down the Avon side of the mountain. The initial descent was deceptively gradual. Starting with a gentle downhill slope, the road quickly got steeper leading into three sharp curves. Several motorists saw Truck 8 swerving over the center line with its driver struggling to maintain control. Carol Winegar, driving up the Avon side of the mountain, saw the truck coming at her around a curve tilting to its left, its right-side wheels off the ground, looking as if it were going to tip over. "It was the craziest thing I ever saw," she said.

Another driver heading up the mountain had a similar thought. "I saw a truck coming down and passing over the center line," said Steve Berry, assistant vice president, The Hartford. "I thought, 'There goes another crazy driver on Avon Mountain.' I just kept going and didn't think anything about it until I got to work and heard the news." Mr. Berry, who would nearly unseat incumbent Thomas Herlihy in an unexpectedly tight race for Connecticut's 8th Senate District in 2006, had a heightened sensitivity to road safety issues. His 16-year-old daughter, Stephanie, had been killed by a drunk driver three years earlier.

Raheem was now picking up even more speed as he headed down Avon Mountain. He stomped on the brake pedal, but that didn't slow him. He pushed the clutch pedal to the floor, but it wouldn't let him downshift into a lower gear. Even if the truck was going slower, getting into a lower gear was probably impossible at that point. A repaired clutch plate was wobbling because the pilot bearing designed to steady it for proper shifting had apparently never been reinstalled. And Truck 8's maxi brake, similar to a car's emergency brake, had deteriorated into a dusty powder spiked with broken springs. Propelled by gravity from descending the steep ridge formed hundreds of millions of years ago, the same ridge that lured today's luxury-house builders and, thus, Truck 8 itself, the only thing Raheem could do was steer.

Truck 8 flew past Geoff Lysaught, who was heading up the mountain. "It was going very fast and I thought it was going to flip over," he said. "It was leaning over so much that its wheels must have just been touching the ground."

By now, Raheem had to be in full terror. His desperate stomping and ramming shattered various truck parts, spewing them all over Avon Mountain near Wright Drive, half a mile from the intersection at the base of the mountain. What about the Jake Brake, which could have slowed him? Did Raheem forget to flip the dashboard switch to activate it? Even if he did activate it, the Jake Brake disengages when the clutch pedal is fully depressed. By now, Truck 8 was going about 70 miles per hour. Within seconds, he was on the last, steep, chute-like straightaway, framed by a blur of the dense green canopy of oak, maple and white pines.

At this point, Raheem could see the crowded intersection ahead. There was no runaway truck lane, no good options. He had a heartbeat in time to make a death-or-maybe-life decision: pull off into the woods to avoid the intersection full of vehicles – almost certain suicide – or hope for a miracle and try to ride it out. Like six other truck drivers in the past 21 years who were suddenly confronted with that very same choice, Raheem chose to ride it out.

Eric Strangefeld, who a minute earlier had passed Raheem just beyond the crest of the mountain, was stopped in the westbound lane at the traffic light at the base of the mountain, looking across the intersection at the 19 eastbound vehicles, most of them waiting to drive uphill. He looked in his rearview mirror and, horrified, saw Truck 8 charging down the hill directly at him.

School bus driver Karen McCall was stopped at the light on Route 10 northbound, preparing to turn her empty bus right onto Route 44 and up the mountain. Her company has a rule against turning right on red, ever. She heard Truck 8 coming. "It was loud, metal on metal, like the sound of heavy rocks violently shaken in an enormous coffee can," she said.

She saw Raheem. "He looked beyond terrified," McCall said. "The truck window was open. He was wearing a white t-shirt with a blue-and-white checkered shirt that was flapping in the wind. He was really concentrating, trying to avoid what was happening. Rocks and sparks were flying out."

Michael Cummings, who had taken a few moments to remove the lawn equipment from the back of his Caravan for a safer trip to work, was near the front of the center-left travel lane. When the light turned from red to green, he shifted his focus from the light and saw the truck. He had time for one thought: "So this is how I'm going to die."

Raheem swerved to his left to avoid Mr. Strangefeld's car and then cut back to his right. In an instant, Truck 8 was tilted up on its driver's side wheels, careening diagonally across the intersection, turned like a battleship delivering a broadside, 35 tons of truck, dirt, gravel, tree stumps and concrete slabs going 80 miles an hour. There was no time to move; nothing to do but brace ourselves, pray or curse. The truck flipped and unleashed its lethal load, violently shoving our vehicles back almost 100 yards – thrusting us into a deadly vortex of slashing, battering, crushing steel and stone.

With its cab and now-empty rear body opened wide in a grasping V-shaped claw, Truck 8 picked off several cars as it slid on its side another 100 screeching, friction-sparked yards past the Kelley Transit bus before its journey ended.

In its wake were utter catastrophe and, for a few moments, eerie silence.

CHAPTER 8

Smoke, Fire and Angels

"Whoso saveth the life of one, it shall be as if
he had saved the life of all mankind."
— *The Koran*

"Whosoever saves one life, saves the world entire."
— *The Talmud*

"Love one another."
— *The Bible*

At 7:38 a.m. on Friday, July 29, 2005, in the shadow of Avon Mountain, a speeding, fully loaded, out-of-control, uninsured Mack dump truck slammed into a cluster of cars and a commuter bus stopped at a red light. Some 30 lives, from near and far and heading in every direction with hopes and dreams and to-do lists, collided and stopped. All but one of us survived the initial impact. Many were hurt, trapped, dying. We needed help. Fast.

They came from north, south, east and west. They came from above. They came in fire trucks, police cars, ambulances and helicopters. They came running from nearby cars, homes and businesses. They came with the latest training and equipment. They came with nothing but their bare hands and humanity. They responded to the sight and sound of steel and earth smashing into thin layers of metal and glass. They responded to hundreds of frantic 911 calls, to the hellish plume of dense black smoke piercing the valley's veneer of tranquility on a beautiful summer day. They came to help total strangers, fellow human beings who so desperately needed them.

More than three hundred firefighters, police, emergency medical workers and passersby answered the hue and cry and descended on the scene. It was chaotic, surreal, incomprehensible, overwhelming. Separate clusters of mangled, smoldering, hissing wrecks stretched out for nearly the length of a football field. Reddish brown dirt and gravel were everywhere, covering everything. In the middle was a Kelley Transit bus, engine still running, transmission in gear, rear wheels churning, cars smashed up against its front and sides. Boulders, slabs of concrete, tree stumps landed in the middle of the road, in cars, on the manicured green grass of Nassau's furniture store. Just beyond the bus was the truck, on its side and starting to burn, load dispersed, tires still spinning. The pungent smell of burning rubber blended with the musty odor of rotting fill. Car alarms wailed. Moans, screams, cursing, crying. Was this Avon or Baghdad? Smoke, more smoke. Fire. Chaos.

The Sound of Velocity

"I simultaneously heard the sound of velocity and looked up and saw the truck," said Richard Frieder, a librarian at the Hartford Public Library. "It was flying. I was looking at the light and had about a second to process it. The truck was starting to tip over, and then impact."

Richard was first in the right-center travel lane, directly to my right. His car, a 1998 Toyota Corolla with 100,000 miles, was sideswiped, which activated the side airbag. His car was pushed to the side, at a 45-degree angle to Nassau's furniture store.

"I kept hearing that truck, the velocity, almost a screaming, then this incredible crashing," he said. "It all happened behind me. I didn't see anything."

Unable to open his dented driver's side door, Richard climbed across the front seat and out the passenger side. He stood outside and looked back behind his car. "Carnage," he said, "and dirt everywhere."

First he called his wife on his cell phone, leaving a message that he was okay. The only thing broken was his watchband. "Then I started walking toward the accident," he said. "I was in shock. There was about a minute of silence. Then the truck blew up."

I Don't Remember

Like Richard, I also had a front-row seat – first row, left-center lane, with nothing between me and the truck – but I don't remember a thing. I don't remember seeing the truck come at me, or the thick slab of concrete launched from the truck's bed, blasting through the windshield and landing on the front passenger seat. I don't remember the other slab of concrete, ripping open my car's roof and landing in the back seat. I don't remember being violently jostled by the force that punctured my left lung and broke my left arm, six ribs and two vertebrae. That same force spun my car like a helicopter blade and left it facing Nassau's, almost perpendicular to the bus.

I don't remember 21-year-old Kyle Caruso, maintenance supervisor at Avon Old Farms Hotel, running from the hotel parking lot to my car and digging frantically with his bare hands through the dirt and gravel that buried me nearly to my chest to find the seat belt release button. At the same time, the Kelley Transit bus, still in gear with tires spinning and smoldering, lurched forward against the demolished, overturned station wagon wedged between my car and the bus.

I don't remember Doug Smith, the Travelers director and Winsted High School wrestling coach, working with Kyle. "What amazed me most," said Doug, "was to see your roof ripped back, to see you buried up to your chest in dirt. There was a slab of concrete in the seat next to you. I was thinking, 'What happened here?' We couldn't open the door. Kyle was digging, trying to get to your seatbelt and I was pulling on the seatbelt while he was taking the dirt out."

Kyle finally pulled me through the crushed driver's side window frame and took me to the safety of Nassau's lawn. "You were moaning, you were in shock," Kyle said. "You wouldn't lie on your back, so we ended up putting you down on your stomach."

I don't remember Lai Shawn Hooks, a receptionist and medical assistant on her way from Hartford to the Avon Medical Group, trying to comfort me as I let loose a profanity-laced mantra as she tried to assess my injuries and get my wife's name and phone number. "You were in shock and shaking really bad, and you were screaming that you were in pain but you couldn't tell us where you were in pain," she said. "You were covered in dirt, so we couldn't see where you were hurt."

I don't remember UConn Health Center firefighter and emergency medical technician (EMT) Tom Clynch taking my vital signs, or Farmington EMT Todd Jensen rolling me over onto my back and determining that I "needed immediate care." I don't remember Farmington firefighter Mike Gulino trying to keep me alert by asking questions. I was within a few yards of the mangled, burning wreckage of 20 vehicles. "I asked if you remembered being in an accident," Mike said. "You said, 'I was in an accident?'" Lights on, but nobody's home. "You had no lung sound on your left side," said Tony Flamio, another Farmington firefighter. "You were in a lot of pain. We didn't like what we were seeing and the way it was going for you. You were turning blue. We wanted to get you out of there quick. Thank God LifeStar was there."

I don't remember my first helicopter ride or the nurses and the pilot who flew me over Avon Mountain, over the morning rush-hour traffic, over my ING office and to-do list, over to a soft landing on the rooftop of Hartford Hospital, where my Friday morning commute finally ended.

I don't remember any of that but, beyond what I've read and been told, I do have a notion – a vague, hazy sense lurking just beneath my consciousness – that something bad happened to me; that I was overwhelmed, trapped, hurt; that I was taken care of. These blurry thoughts sometimes flicker into feelings of déjà vu, sparked by certain faces and traffic situations, all connected to the morning of July 29, 2005.

Final Tragic Journey

We'll never know if Maureen Edlund saw it coming. The office worker with a passion for painting, the devoted single mom of Tara and care-giving daughter of Margaret, was about to turn left onto Nod Road, the scenic and tranquil part of her morning journey. Her 2001 Buick Century was the first car hit directly by Truck 8. The impact killed her.

Truck 8 was not finished. The 50,000 pounds of rough fill that it launched at 80 miles per hour set off a cyclone of smashing vehicles. Barbara Bongiovanni, who steadfastly stood by wayward son Vincent, tak-ing care of him and her elderly, Alzheimer's-afflicted mother Carmella, was three cars behind me in the left center lane. The force squeezed her 2000 Chrysler out into the far left lane and directly into the path of the overturned sliding truck which had already ensnared Maureen Edlund's car. The two caregivers who were on remarkably similar life journeys – suffering the early deaths of their husbands 14 years earlier, leaving both to raise nine-year-old children alone – were now on a final tragic path to-gether. The truck dragged their cars along the pavement for nearly a hun-dred yards, before finally stopping. Then it burst into flames. Maureen and Barbara, these highly responsible, loving and beloved ladies, died "as a direct result of this collision," according to Connecticut's chief medical examiner – Maureen of "blunt trauma injuries" and Barbara of "smoke inhalation."[1]

Truck driver Abdulraheem Naafi, on the very last part of his own twist-ing and difficult earthly voyage – who was trying to turn his life around and just wanted to drive trucks – was trapped with a badly broken leg inside the cab of Truck 8. He struggled desperately to free himself after the truck finally slid to a stop. As Raheem screamed for help, diesel fuel leaked from the truck's ruptured tanks. Before anyone could help him – and several tried – small spark-ignited flames exploded into a ghastly ball of intense fire, generating a column of heavy black smoke that rose high into the clear blue summer sky.

"I could not get to him," said Dr. Scott Kurtzman, the head of surgery at Waterbury Hospital who had gotten a five-minute head start that morning because of a shorter-than-usual walk with his dog. As the accident unfold-ed, he was behind the bus as he approached the backed-up traffic. When he saw the truck up on its side and about to flip over, he pulled sharply to his right, up over the curb and onto the lawn of Nassau's. "The flames were just too intense to get him," Dr. Kurtzman said. "It was impossible." According to the medical examiner, Raheem died of "smoke inhalation and thermal injury as a direct result of this collision."[2]

---

1. Arrest Warrant Application, p. 7, paragraph 1
2. Arrest Warrant Application, p. 7, paragraph 4

Angels

She heard it before she saw it. Dr. Elena Tomasi, the dentist from Belarus who was wearing her new black-and-white blouse and who had spent a little extra time on her hair that morning, had just passed the Kelley Transit bus as she approached the base of Avon Mountain. Not wanting to be stuck behind a slow-moving bus going up the steep grade of Avon Mountain, she had maneuvered her small, blue, box-shaped, 1993 Dodge Spirit into the right travel lane, directly in front of Frank Juan and his Kelley Transit bus.

"I heard a bump. I heard the sound first," Dr. Tomasi said. "The truck hit a car, but it seemed so far from me that I thought, 'I will be a witness to an accident.'" She saw the truck flip and start hitting more cars. "Then I saw a vehicle moving towards me – 'oh sh--!' Those are the only two words I remember because I [had been] absolutely sure that they weren't going to hit me; I was so far in the back. And then there was a gray wall or something coming and closing the view." It was a Subaru Outback station wagon, now airborne. "I remember gray and dust, no pain, no nothing," Dr. Tomasi said. "I didn't feel anything...and then I remember dreaming about the accident."

In the maelstrom of colliding vehicles, a sharp edge from her smashed car ripped along the driver's side of the bus. Dr. Tomasi was dazed and bleeding heavily from a head wound. Her car finally stopped within a few yards of the overturned, burning truck.

Todd Myers, the volunteer firefighter and off-duty West Hartford cop, who just minutes earlier had taken an extra 30 seconds to check his voice-mail in his Simsbury driveway, saw the accident unfold from about a hundred yards away. "I saw a huge cloud of dirt," he said. "I saw the brake lights on the bus. It was drifting right, and then the truck caught fire. All this happened in seconds. It was too much to process that quickly."

He pulled his truck off onto the right shoulder of Route 44. He grabbed his portable radio and backpack and started running toward the smoke and fire. He had no time to put on the firefighting gear in his trunk over his white t-shirt and shorts. While running, he called the West Hartford police dispatch. "I need help!" he screamed into the radio, explaining that there was a massive crash at the base of Avon Mountain. An enormous emergency-services response was now gearing up, but it would be precious minutes before the first fire truck arrived.

He went to Dr. Tomasi first. "The heat from the truck and fire was phenomenal," he said. "I couldn't get to the truck driver. I ended up on the passenger side of Elena's car and I was yanking on the door. She was in and out of consciousness." Officer Myers wasn't able to get the damaged door open so he ran to the other side. At this point, the back of her car caught fire. "There was dirt everywhere," Officer Myers said. "I threw handfuls of dirt to smother the flames. Five people were standing on the grass watching. I'm yelling for them to help me. One guy said, 'C'mon, let's help!'"

But within seconds, the fire had spread. "I reached in and tried pulling her," he said, burning his left arm in the process. "But she had her seat belt on." Within the mangled car, the seat belt release button was inaccessible. Dr. Tomasi, 5'4" and 115 pounds, was trapped.

"I see the dream and I want to wake up, but I can't," Dr. Tomasi said. "It was really an unpleasant feeling. The dream was people rushing, yelling, screaming – I just wanted it to end. Then I noticed somebody in my car trying to talk to me. I remember somebody wearing white. And I don't know why, but I was thinking about angels. And why are they in my car? What are they doing in my car?"

Officer Myers was back at the passenger-side window. By this time, Dr. Kurtzman was on the driver's side. The Dodge Spirit was on fire, just yards away from the burning truck and the crash's first three fatalities. Then something else exploded on the truck. "A massive wave of heat shifted our way," Officer Myers said. "It was really hot." Dr. Tomasi was still trapped. The fire was advancing on her. Then Officer Meyers remembered his knife. He reached into his pocket and pulled out the six-inch, jet-black, razor-sharp *Benchmade* utility knife that he always carried with him. He flipped it to Dr. Kurtzman, who was at the driver's door which was jammed shut. "I cut her seatbelt, there was no other way to get it off," Dr. Kurtzman said. "The mechanism was jammed in. There was no way to get to it."

"Todd Myers kept saying, 'Crawl to me!'" Dr. Tomasi said. "I couldn't respond, so he brought his arm around me because the car was already on fire."

With broken glass embedded in his hands and his left arm already scorched, with only his thin white t-shirt for protection, Officer Myers again reached into the burning car with both arms and yanked for dear life. "I grabbed her by her shirt and hair, whatever I could get a hold of," he said. "And I pulled in one big motion. Some other guy came over and helped me carry her to the grass."

Officer Myers and Eric Tully, a passing motorist who just missed being hit by the truck, carried her to the green lawn of Nassau's, her dark red blood soaking the new black-and-white blouse. She was still dazed, still bleeding, still alive. The rescuers, her angels, looked back to see her car fully engulfed in flames.

Command and Control

Fire Chief James "Jamie" DiPace had responded to thousands of calls during his 33 years of service with the Avon Volunteer Fire Department. During that entire time, there was not one single fire-related death in Avon. Chief DiPace had no way of knowing that, as he tossed a Frisbee to his dog just outside the back door of his Avon house, the decades-long streak had ended minutes earlier, that fiery death had barreled down the mountain and devastated dozens of lives in the valley.

"I'm keen to certain sounds, and one of them is the sound of my pager," Chief DiPace said. The message was from his assistant fire chief – bad accident at the base of Avon Mountain. As Chief DiPace got closer to the scene, he saw the towering plume of black smoke. "At first I thought it might be an airplane," he said. Low-flying commercial airliners on their descent into nearby Bradley International Airport routinely fly over the valley. "I drove up onto the lawn of the furniture store and saw a huge rock – very strange. I had never seen that rock before, and I've passed by there hundreds of times."

He was looking for a place to set up a command position. "We had three separate incidents going on," he said. "Fire, extrication and medical. My biggest concern was for the injured."

His assistant chief, Peter Delap, was already at the scene, which was just down the road from his regular full-time job as supervisor for the Connecticut Department of Transportation (DOT).

"I was sitting in my office talking on my Nextel [radio] to one of my fire captains, and the dispatcher starts saying there's a major accident," Asst. Chief Delap said. "Then all of the sudden, my two-way radio pings. It's a guy I work with at the DOT, Aaron. He said he was at the bottom of the mountain in a bad accident. I told another guy I work with that Aaron was in a bad accident. He said, 'I'm going with you.' A lot of the guys down here are pretty tight. I pull out and say, 'It can't be that bad, you know?' I didn't hear the initial dispatch. All I know is that there's an accident. As I pull out on Waterville Road, the traffic is backing up, so I put the siren on. Then I see this big column of black smoke. I thought, 'That's not good.' I came around the corner and said, 'holy sh--!' It's like something out of a Bruce Willis movie."

He crossed through the intersection onto Route 44 and pulled his pickup truck, with its trailer carrying lawnmower equipment still attached, to the shoulder of the road. He saw Officer Todd Meyers pointing to a crushed, overturned car and yelling that someone was trapped. "The dump truck was burning, but I couldn't get out of my truck because I had to call for help. We needed more resources. I had to set things up. That's my job," Asst. Chief Delap said. He radioed for both "LifeStars," the medical transport helicopters from Hartford Hospital. He couldn't get through to the Avon dispatcher, who was overwhelmed with 911 calls. He turned to his second radio, a lower frequency, to contact neighboring Farmington.

"They couldn't understand why I was calling if the accident was in Avon," he said. By now, his pager had alerted his fire department boss, Chief DiPace. After that, he put on his firefighting gear and ran to the overturned car, wedged between my car and the Kelley Transit bus.

By this time, Avon Police Chief Peter Agnesi had arrived at the crash site. "In 28 years on the job, I had never seen anything like this," he said. "What struck me was that it was one very large scene, but several individual areas needed immediate attention."

The emergency services leaders, DiPace and Agnesi, were working together to set up a command post. "It was chaos," Chief Agnesi said. "We were trying to gain some control over what we had, assess it, and call in additional assistance from the region. The first thing we did was to set up a triage area by the side of Nassau's for the injured."

Left for Dead

One second, Travelers executive and Kelley Transit bus passenger Doug Smith was working on his laptop computer, and the next he and his computer were on the floor. "I heard the bus driver yell, 'What the hell!' I looked up and saw something large coming at the bus," Doug said. "I was thrown to the floor. I had papers; who knows where they went. There was a first impact that jarred us back and a second impact that really launched the bus backwards. The accelerator pedal was stuck. As soon as the second impact took place, it ripped the whole driver's side of the bus open and he [Frank Juan, the bus driver] fell off to the side, down where the stairs are."

That second impact was the Subaru Outback, which had been propelled upward and into the windshield. With the bus's accelerator pedal stuck and transmission still in gear, the rear tires were spinning and smoldering. "The bus filled up with smoke," Doug said. "It went forward a ways before it finally stopped. We couldn't get to Frank because the bar behind the driver's seat was blocking the aisle. I opened one of the emergency windows, grabbed my laptop and went out the window."

He glanced behind, expecting other passengers to follow. "After I got out of the bus, I looked around," Doug said. "I didn't know if we had been bombed or what happened. Just to see the dirt and debris all over the road. I couldn't imagine where it all came from. It was like a bomb went off and just blew dirt and tree stumps all over the road. It was like a war zone." Another Travelers manager and bus passenger, Ed Giarnese, started helping people through the emergency window, and Doug helped them down from the outside. "I was yelling, 'Get out, get out!' The bus was still trying to go forward. It was smoking. I was afraid it was going to go up in flames."

There was only one person left on Bus 200 – its driver, Frank Juan, slumped lifelessly off the driver's seat and onto the floor. Ed remembered once watching Frank open the door from the outside by opening a spring-loaded cover to the right of the door and flipping the toggle switch. The door opened and Ed, Doug and Officer Todd Myers teamed up to help Frank.

The norm for critically injured accident victims is to handle them with the utmost delicacy because of the possibility of spinal fractures. With the bus's rear tires spinning and smoking heavily, this was not an option for Frank Juan. "We thought the bus was about to go up in flames," Ed said. They wanted to get him away from the immediate peril of fire. Officer Myers grabbed Frank and, with help from Ed and Doug, carried him down the three stairs of the bus and onto the Nassau's lawn. "He had a big gash from ear to ear," Doug said. "He was unconscious; he wasn't responding."

It didn't look good for Frank, who was supposed to escort his daughter, Ramona, down the aisle on her wedding day in 43 days. He lay uncon-scious on the ground, neck broken, not breathing. Officer Myers said, "He was dead when we turned him over to the paramedics."

Emergency services people started to arrive. Firefighter/paramedics Tom Clynch and Victor Morrone drove up in the Rescue 2 truck from the UConn Health Center Fire Department. "It was obvious that it was an MCI [mass casualty incident]," Victor said. "We called the North Central Coordination Center, which alerts hospitals and controls which patients go where. We're used to chaos, but this was different. We couldn't see the end of the accident. It looked like it was stretched out for about 200 yards. There was nothing we could do for the truck driver and the people near the truck. The Avon and West Hartford police guided us to who was still alive." And that did not include Frank Juan. At that point, the rescuers had left him for dead.

"In a mass casualty incident, you don't normally pick out people who don't look like they're going to survive," Tom Clynch said, as he explained the need to triage, to allocate treatment to those with the greatest chance to live. "I don't know, for some reason we wanted to try to give him a chance. So we ventilated him, gave him a good airway, put the bag valve mask on him." But by now, the bus looked like it was going to fully ignite.

"We already had chaos," Tom said. "There were other cars jammed up against the bus with people in them. If we had a full-blown bus fire…" He dropped everything, grabbed a 2.5-gallon fire extinguisher off an Avon fire truck and went after the burning tires. "Someone else brought over another one, and we knocked [the fire] down," Tom said. And finally, someone was able to get by the debris blocking the driver's area of the bus to reach over to the ignition key and turn it off.

By now, Dr. Kurtzman was working on Frank who showed no signs of life. He had help from Registered Nurse Paula Pileski, who was on her way from the night shift at Hartford Hospital to her home in West Simsbury. "He looked bad," she said. "I didn't know how he was going to survive." They worked together to perform cardio-pulmonary resuscitation (CPR). Dr. Kurtzman inserted a breathing tube into Frank's windpipe. Nurse Pileski ventilated Frank while Dr. Kurtzman did chest compressions. Finally, a pulse returned. A LifeStar helicopter landed, and its medical crew continued to work on Frank during the five-minute flight to Hartford Hospital.

Against daunting odds, Frank Juan was still alive, body badly broken but spirit intact. He would need that fighting spirit and the strong support of his loving family to face the difficult battles to come.

A Final Thought

Michael Cummings, the IT supervisor at St. Francis Hospital who was wary of the mountain between his job and new home in New Hartford, who had removed lawn equipment from his Dodge Caravan earlier that morning, literally assumed his life was over. He was near the front of the line of traffic waiting at the light at the intersection, and had a clear view of what was bearing down on us.

"Cars were coming up behind me and on either side of me, and when the light turned green I was looking at the light," Michael said. "I looked down when it turned green, and that's when I saw the truck coming through the intersection."

Two cars heading in the same direction as the truck were stopped at the light, preparing to turn right onto Nod Road. Michael saw the truck swerve to avoid them and tilt up on its driver's side wheels. "All this happened within a second," Michael said. "I'm guessing he was doing 100 miles an hour. It was extremely loud."

He saw a panicked Abdulraheem Naafi trying to steer the out-of-control truck, which was headed right at him. "Oh my God, I'm dead," Michael said to himself. "I remember feeling, 'So this is how it happens; you just never know how you're going to die.' I just bit down and closed my eyes," he said. "I guess he swerved just enough to miss me, but all the dirt and debris hit my car and pushed it back pretty far. Then I was hit by the Kelley Transit bus from behind, which pushed me into another lane while I was t-boned by a white car."

Hammered from all sides, Michael was knocked unconscious. The next thing he remembered was a rescuer telling him to wake up, that there was a bad fire and that he needed to get out of his minivan. "I was pretty surprised because I thought I was dead," he said. "I had no doubt in my mind that it was over."

From a pain perspective, Michael's story was just beginning. Among the rescuers who extricated him from his demolished minivan was UConn Health Center firefighter/paramedic Victor Morrone. "We're going to move you, and it's going to hurt," he told Michael. Badly battered and bruised, his injuries included broken ribs, a broken collarbone and an excruciatingly painful, severely broken right arm. With those injuries and the mangled condition of his minivan, it was a difficult, painful extrication. Victor and his emergency services colleagues finally managed to get him out and onto the safety of Nassau's lawn.

"He had a really bad compound fracture," said Dr. Kurtzman. "It was at right angles."

After helping me and Dr. Tomasi, Lai Shawn Hooks, the receptionist and medical assistant from Avon Medical Group, was now helping Dr. Kurtzman with Michael. "He had broken everything," she said. "He was very badly injured. Dr. Kurtzman rolled up his sleeves and went right at it. He didn't think about malpractice or anything. He just did what he had to do."

As the head of surgery at Waterbury Hospital and with decades of hands-on experience, Dr. Kurtzman was well aware of the full range of potential medical and legal issues. But his overriding focus this morning was simply on helping people. "You just have to do the right thing and not worry about being in a litigious society," he said. "Some attorneys might tell you something different. But screw that, we can't live our lives that way."

While Dr. Kurtzman worked on stabilizing Michael and resetting his badly broken arm, Lai Shawn contacted Michael's wife, Tammy, who just minutes earlier had said her daily morning prayer for her husband as she drove to her job in Simsbury. "I wanted to call my wife because I didn't want her to hear about this from anyone else," Michael said. "If she heard me, she'd know that I'd be alright."

Lai Shawn called Tammy. "It wasn't a call that you'd ever want to get," Tammy said. "I was just going through my regular routine driving to work. I always say a prayer on my way to work. I had just finished praying, and that's when my cell phone rang. It was a woman asking, 'Do you know a Mike?' She said he has been in a very bad accident, he definitely had a broken arm, he had a pulse, and he was breathing on his own. I was comforted, the fact that she called. It was scary, and it was a horrible call, but just to hear that he was okay...when I think of all the scenarios of how I could have found out, that was the best way. I was very grateful."

Lai Shawn handed the phone to Michael and told him to tell Tammy that he loved her. "You don't know for sure what's going to happen," Lai Shawn said. "You never know if it's going to be your last...at least she would have that much."

Dr. Kurtzman also talked with Tammy. "It was a little bizarre," he said. "Her husband's lying there injured, and now she knows about it. I told her he was going to be okay. She wanted to know where he was going to be taken. I wasn't sure. So I wrote her name and phone number on his chest and circled it so that when he got to the hospital someone would call her."

Michael had left his new home in New Hartford 45 minutes earlier, heading to his job at Saint Francis Hospital. He eventually got there, but for a much different reason than originally intended.

It would be at least another hour or so before Dr. Kurtzman would leave the scene. There was still work to do – another person was trapped and in dire need of help.

Evidence

In the age of cell phones, emails and electronic media, news of the crash instantly reverberated throughout the Farmington Valley and Greater Hartford vicinity. Friends and family members immediately began checking in with one another. It seemed that virtually everyone in the area was either one of the 23,000 daily commuters passing through the intersection at the base of Avon Mountain, or knew someone who was. People needed to hear the voices of loved ones.

"Something terrible happened. Life was reduced to its essentials. People said what counted, what mattered," wrote Peggy Noonan, best-selling author and former presidential speechwriter, about the immediate aftermath of 9-11. "It has been noted that there is no record of anyone calling to say, 'I never liked you,' or 'You hurt my feelings.' No one negotiated past grievances or said, 'Vote for Smith'...No one said anything unneeded, extraneous or small. Crisis is a great editor."[3]

People wanted basic information. Are you okay? What happened? How many dead? Injured? How serious? Who were they? Who was the truck driver? Who owned the truck? The entire area soon became fixated on the intersection at the base of Avon Mountain.

Avon Police Captain Mark Rinaldo (currently Avon Chief of Police) was on his way down the mountain at the time of the crash. "I was behind the accident by a couple of minutes," he said. He was on his way from his South Windsor home to an Avon Rotary Club meeting at Avon Old Farms Hotel at the base of the mountain. He was running a few minutes late. He had forgotten to walk his three cocker spaniels, so he had returned home.

---

3. *Wall Street Journal*, "I Just Called to Say I Love You," Peggy Noonan, March 10, 2007

By the time Capt. Rinaldo reached Avon Mountain, he knew a crash had occurred. But he didn't know how bad it was until he came down the Avon side of the mountain and saw a terrible sight unfold before him. "The road was blocked. The truck was on fire. It was just a bunch of cars...it was terrible. I've never seen anything that devastating or of that magnitude."

Capt. Rinaldo went into "auto pilot" and focused on what needed to be done. "I wanted to make sure we had enough resources, and coordinate what was going on," he said. Emergency services workers, the media, good Samaritans and the curious were all descending on the scene. "We had to maintain control," he said, "and protect anything that might be needed as evidence for the crash investigation."

As part of the effort to control the scene and guard potential evidence, Avon Mountain was shut down to traffic. That was a big problem for West Hartford resident Dan Jones, an awarding-winning journalist who covered Avon for the *Hartford Courant*. He had graduated first in his class from the Columbia University Graduate School of Journalism, and had written about everything from homicide to the environment during his 22 years of newspaper work. He had also covered seemingly endless routine town government meetings during his time reporting on Avon events. Now the most spectacular story of his Avon tenure was breaking – right this very minute – and he was stopped cold by a West Hartford patrol officer who was not allowing traffic onto Route 44 on the West Hartford side of Avon Mountain. How would he ever show his face in the newsroom again if he couldn't get to the biggest Avon news story in decades?

"I had to get there," Dan said. "I told her that if I didn't get this story, I was going to be in a lot of trouble. Finally, she said okay." Even with all his reporting experience, Dan was shocked by what he saw as he descended the Avon side of the mountain. "I have never seen anything like it," he said. "It looked like somebody had bombed the bus because part of it was open, vehicles were smashed. I thought to myself, 'This is a major disaster.'"

By now, Capt. Rinaldo had sectioned off the media to a patch of grass on the north side of Route 44. Dan squinted at the truck's license plate. He was too far away to see it clearly. He asked a cameraman from a local TV station to zoom in on it. There it was: Connecticut commercial license plate J67870. Dan called it into his *Hartford Courant* colleagues back at the main office on Broad Street in Hartford. They plugged it into the Department of Motor Vehicles (DMV) data base. Bingo. The computer screen lit up with the truck's owner, American Crushing & Recycling (ACR) from Bloomfield, and its long history of hundreds of safety violations. The company's president was listed as David R. Wilcox.

Noel Janovic, a technical assistant at Webster Insurance of Waterford, Conn., had a voicemail message awaiting her when she arrived at work at 9:00 a.m. Donna Wilcox, an ACR administrative assistant and wife of David Wilcox, had left her a message at 8:20 a.m., less than an hour after ACR's Truck 8 crashed at the base of Avon Mountain. She asked about the status of the liability coverage on all 12 ACR dump trucks. At this point, one driver was still trapped in his demolished car. The bodies of Maureen Edlund, Barbara Bongiovanni and ACR employee Abdulraheem Naafi had yet to be removed from their charred vehicles. Six months earlier, it was Donna Wilcox who had called Noel to cancel the liability insurance on all 12 ACR dump trucks, a call that resulted in a $39,976 credit to ACR. At 9:05 a.m., before Noel had a chance to check the ACR coverage status and return the call, Mrs. Wilcox was on the phone again. After Noel confirmed that the liability insurance had indeed been suspended in January, Mrs. Wilcox said she wanted to reinstate full coverage on all 12 vehicles, retroactively, as of July 1, 2005. And she wanted written confirmation that the coverage had been reinstated. It wasn't until later that morning, not until her fourth call to Webster Insurance, that Mrs. Wilcox mentioned that an ACR truck had been involved in a fatal crash a few hours earlier.

Slipping the Surly Bonds

> One summer day, the elf students and teachers arrived to the school but the giant wasn't there. It was not like him to be late. In fact, he was usually the first one at the school…A few of the elf teachers had heard a loud crash coming from upstream earlier that morning…[4]

The arithmetic and physics say that 70,000 pounds of truck and earth going 80 miles an hour will produce approximately 15 million pounds of energy, which translates into about 10 sticks of dynamite. How does a force that massive disperse when it collides with 19 vehicles stopped at a traffic light? The physical damage would eventually be measured, quantified and chronicled. But as fires were doused and smoke dissipated, it was becoming all too clear that the emotional havoc and heartbreak wrought by David Wilcox's Truck 8 would be beyond calculation.

Chip Stotler, a special education teacher and father of five little girls, was in the second row of traffic in the right center travel lane, just in front of Elena Tomasi, who was in front of Frank Juan and his Kelley Transit bus. As Truck 8 careened diagonally across the intersection and flipped over, releasing 25 tons of rough fill at a high speed, the force propelled a cluster of cars into a torrent of crashing, battering steel, glass, dirt and stone. Chip's Subaru Outback station wagon was first squeezed into a frame-bending arc, then launched into the windshield of the bus.

---

4. Excerpts from "A Fairy Tale," by John Drewry, one of Chip Stotler's Gengras Center colleagues.

It landed on its roof, just behind my car, and was leaning into the front of the still-running bus. Frank Juan, unconscious with a broken neck, still had his foot on the bus's accelerator. The rear tires dug in and smoldered, pushing against the Outback. Inside, trapped and critically wounded, Chip was held by his seatbelt and pinned by the "B-post," the part of the door frame to which the seat belt is attached. It was now bent across his chest.

"I knew this was going to require an extended extrication," said Pete Delap, Avon's assistant fire chief. "I called for the UConn [University of Connecticut Health Center] technical rescue." In order to talk to Chip, Asst. Chief Delap had to lie flat on his stomach to see into the overturned car. "I told him, 'We're going to get you out of here.'"

It wasn't going to be easy. There was the immediate menace of the bus, rear wheels churning and on the verge of igniting the entire vehicle, which was still pushing forward into Chip's flattened car. Getting inside that compressed space to Chip would be extremely difficult. And the car was upside down. The relatively simple procedure of cutting through the car's roof was not an option at this point. And cutting into the more hardened, crumpled steel of other parts of the car would also be difficult.

"We had to make sure the car wasn't going to fall as soon as we took off the parts that were holding him," said Tim Vibert, chief, Farmington Volunteer Fire Department, and owner of Farmington Motor Sports, a local vehicle repair and towing company. He was working with Bill Perkins, chief of the UConn rescue team, who was leading the extrication effort. Some two dozen rescuers began the painstaking and time-consuming process of jacking up the Outback with airbags and cribbing; blocks of varying sizes were placed under the car as it was slowly elevated.

In addition to the extrication activity, rescuers attended to Chip's medical needs as best they could in the cramped space. Victor Morrone, the UConn firefighter/paramedic who helped extricate Michael Cummings, also helped Chip. "If we find you alive, we're going to keep you alive," Victor said, voicing the rescuers' intense desire to achieve their overarching goal. "I told Chip repeatedly that we were going to get him out of there."

Rob Magao was on regular patrol in his West Hartford Police cruiser. He heard fellow officer Todd Myers' radio call for help. Rob took off over the mountain, going from West Hartford to Avon in only a few moments. He gasped as he headed down the Avon side of the mountain. "It looked like a war zone," he said. "I saw people on the Nassau's lawn standing there with their hands over their mouths as Todd was pulling someone from a burning car. He told me to look for other victims. The truck and a few cars were on fire...it was one of the worst things I've ever seen." Only 33 years old, Rob had already seen more than most do in a lifetime. Seven months earlier, he was part of the regional police SWAT (special weapons and tactics) team that was fired at by a drunken gunman who had already killed Peter Lavery, a Newington police officer. Five years earlier, Rob had been present after East Hartford Police Officer Brian Aselton was shot and killed by a robbery suspect.

Following Todd Myers' request, Rob began looking for other victims. "As I was running to help Todd, I saw a car in front of the bus that was upside down," he said. "It was a wreck." The bus's engine continued to rev and a LifeStar helicopter hovered nearby. "I called in and asked what his name was. It was very loud from the bus and all the chaos, so I had to ask him three or four times. He was very patient with me. He said, 'My name is Paul, but they call me Chip.'"

Rob was surprised that externally Chip didn't look badly injured. "I could see his face," Rob said. "He had some trauma, but not what I expected to see by looking at the car."

With all the other rescuers working on the extrication, Rob decided that the best way to help Chip was to crawl into the car to be with him. But gas was leaking all over the Outback, and the bus appeared to be on the verge of catching fire. Avon Police Sergeant T. J. Jacius told Rob to get out of the car.

"I could smell smoke but couldn't see any fire," Rob said. "I told Chip I wouldn't leave him. I was holding his hand, and put the oxygen mask on him." Eventually Chip wanted the mask off. Rob removed it. "He didn't have any problem talking," Rob said. "He said he felt claustrophobic. I asked him if he had family. He said, "Yes, a wife and five kids." Most of their conversation involved Rob monitoring how Chip was doing and explaining the rescue effort that was under way. "He knew that a large truck had made impact," Rob said. "He saw the truck coming and said that he couldn't move and didn't know what to do, that he had no time."

As they talked, Rob worried about how they were going to get Chip out. "It was such a mangled mess," Rob said. "So many things were pinning him in. At first, I couldn't tell the front of the car from the back."

Rob comforted Chip as the other rescuers surrounded the car, working feverishly to elevate it. Someone was finally able to turn off the bus. It was then pulled backward, giving the rescuers more room to work. As the car was being elevated, Tim Vibert was trying to figure out which hydraulic tools he would need to free Chip.

While all this activity was taking place, the conversation inside the car continued. "Are you okay?" Chip asked Rob. "You should get out of the car – listen to the firemen. I'm here because I have to be. Why are you here?" Rob was dumbfounded. Here was this critically injured man, pinned tightly in his demolished car, and he was worried about *him*. "Very few times when you help people do they exhibit much care for you," Rob said. "Chip was in a very difficult position, but he was concerned with my safety over his own. He never complained."

Rob was initially optimistic about getting Chip out. "Once I realized he was talking to me, I thought as long as he can hold on, they'll eventually pull this thing apart. It will just take some time," Rob said. "But as it went on and on, it seemed like forever."

By this time, except for Chip, the disposition of all the other people in the path of Truck 8 had been settled; they either had been treated and transported to Saint Francis Hospital, Hartford Hospital or the University of Connecticut Health Center in Farmington, or they were deceased. Dr. Kurtzman and other medical personnel, including the crew of a LifeStar helicopter, were standing by, ready and waiting to help Chip. "We were prepared," Dr. Kurtzman said. "We had about 10 minutes to get ready for him. We were just standing around, waiting. Everyone else had been taken care of. One person was assigned to put a tube in. One was assigned to listen to vital signs. We were ready to do all those things."

After about 45 minutes, the Outback had been elevated enough for Tim Vibert to begin using a large, heavy hydraulic cutting tool called a saw-all to get at Chip. Ultimately, the rescuers removed nearly half the car. "He was thinking about his family," Rob said.

The extrication effort had reached the point where Rob had to get out of the car. Other rescuers needed to get inside so they could work at freeing Chip. "I told Chip I had to get out," Rob said. "I told him I'd be right outside, and that LifeStar was waiting for him. He said 'thank you' a bunch of times for being with him and not leaving him."

Jeff Hogan, deputy chief, Farmington Volunteer Fire Department and regional manager for Rogers Benefit Group, was in a business suit and just about to leave his Farmington home to give a sales presentation in Shelton, Conn. But then he heard the call for help on his pager, dropped everything, and headed for the crash scene. Before long, he was shimmying into the car on his back to help Tim get Chip out. In his spare time, Jeff hits the gym, including Saturday mornings at the Valley Fitness Center in Unionville where an informal group of guys lifts weights together. Jeff is among those who routinely bench press over 400 pounds. He was going to need that strength.

Tim began cutting at the last few pieces of metal holding Chip. "I was upside down, trying to cut one more piece of metal," Tim said. Sweating profusely, Tim and Jeff worked fiercely to free Chip. Still, the B-post was pinning him in. "I grabbed that last piece of metal with all my might," Jeff said, "and that's when he was finally freed." Tim pulled Chip out and into the waiting arms of the medical crew.

"We put him on a back board and hurried him to LifeStar," said Victor Morrone, the UConn paramedic. During that short walk, as he helped carry

Chip to the helicopter, Victor's shoulders began to sag. "We usually save people," he said. "I realized that Chip was probably not going to make it."

No one can say with certainty exactly where and when Chip Stotler died. It could have been at the scene of the crash. It could have been at Hartford Hospital, where he was officially declared dead. Or it could have been in the LifeStar helicopter en route to the hospital as it flew over Chip's Gengras Center colleagues in West Hartford and the playground he built for his special elves.

Oh! I have slipped the surly bonds of Earth
And danced the skies on laughter-silvered wings;
Sunward I've climbed and joined the tumbling mirth of sun-split clouds…

…Up, up the long, delirious, burning blue
I've topped the wind-swept heights with easy grace
Where never lark, nor even eagle flew –
And, while with silent lifting mind I've trod
The high, untrespassed sanctity of space,
Put out my hand and touched the face of God.[5]

---

5. Excerpted from the poem "High Flight," by John Gillespie Magee, Jr. (1922-1941); born in Shanghai, China; pilot in Royal Canadian Air Force; attended Avon Old Farms School, Avon, Conn., 3 miles from intersection of Nod Road and Routes 44 and 10.

PART 2

The Aftermath

CHAPTER 9

"Please Don't Go Yet"

All bets were off for those called to emergency rooms looking for loved ones. After all, the day had begun like so many others. There was no warning, no reason to believe that this day would not unfold like the thousands before it – wake up, go to work, come home to our families. That would be the first shattered assumption, the first searing realization: We unwittingly take for granted the very things we treasure most. By mid morning, virtually everyone in the greater Hartford area knew of the horrific crash at the base of Avon Mountain. And by then, a few dozen had received the dreaded phone call: Go to the emergency room right away.

That's about all they knew as they dropped everything to start the frantic drive to the ER – that their loved one was hurt and that he or she was at the hospital. And that's when the pleading and bargaining and praying began: Please God let him live. Yes, there's been a terrible crash, and yes people were hurt badly, but she made it to the hospital. Surely with all of today's ultra-modern technology and highly skilled medical experts, surely if he was seriously hurt, surely they can put her back together. Just patch him up and we'll take it from there. At the very least, Dear God, even if she has some debilitating injury, we can handle that, we'll take care of him. Please, Dear God, please let my husband/wife/daughter/son/father/mother/sister/brother/friend live.

On this morning in the emergency rooms of John Dempsey, Saint Francis and Hartford Hospitals, some prayers were answered, and some were not.

✧ ✧ ✧ ✧

"What happened?" I asked groggily.

"Dude, I don't know," the doctor replied.[1]

Dr. Ronald I. Gross was not my father's doctor. Balding and cowboy booted with a confidence-inspiring knowing smile, 54-year-old Dr. Gross was 5'9" of can-do swagger. Two years earlier, he was stationed just outside Baghdad, putting broken U.S. soldiers and Iraqi children back together again.

It was a situation he pursued. "This is what I do for a living," he told a friend in the Pentagon. "I need you to find a forward surgical position and put me there because that's where I belong. It's my obligation to take care of that. These are American soldiers and they deserve the best medical

---

1. *Hartford Courant*, July 30, 2005, Carolyn Moreau, p. 1, "One Man's Commute To Emergency Room"

care possible. If I'm good enough to do it here [in Hartford], I figured I sure as hell am good enough to do it there. My goal was to go over there and send at least one of our men or women home on a stretcher who otherwise would've gone back in a box."

Dr. Gross achieved that goal, and not just for American soldiers. "Four kids were playing in a field, hit a mine and blew up," he said. "One had his bowels hanging out and a piece of shrapnel torn through his jaw and into his head. Another had a shattered pelvis and was also eviscerated." Against all odds, Dr. Gross and his medical team saved them, winning over the virulently anti-American mother of the most grievously wounded. "She tried pairing me up with one of the gals in her village," Dr. Gross said. "When she found out that I was recently engaged, she decided she wanted to come to the States to cook for my wedding."

Of course, many of his wartime experiences did not have happy endings. He couldn't save Sgt. Bobby Franklin, a 39-year-old National Guard soldier, father of two, who upon seeing a roadside bomb turned his Hummer to shield fellow soldiers from the blast while he took the full impact. Talking to Sgt. Franklin's wife on the phone was one of the hardest things Dr. Gross ever had to do. "We talked for about an hour," he said. "We both ended up crying and laughing, just a flood of emotions. But I realized that, at the very least, I had given her some closure. Sometimes that's all you can do."

Upon his return to Hartford Hospital, where he was associate director of traumatology and assistant professor of surgery, life once again settled into a fairly normal routine, at least as normal as it gets for a trauma surgeon. And so it was on that morning in late July, until Dr. Gross took a call from a nurse in the emergency room.

"There's a bad crash on Avon Mountain," he recalled her saying. "And there's all sorts of hell breaking loose."

"Are you there?" Chris, my wife, emailed me from her office in Farmington Town Hall where she was assistant tax collector. She had already called my office several times. No answer. At 8:35 a.m., about an hour after the crash, Lee Beckwith, administrative assistant to Farmington Town Manager Kathy Eagen, received a phone call. A year earlier, Lee and her family were seriously injured in a terrible car crash while on vacation in Aruba. The call brought back a rash of difficult memories as Lee hurried from her desk to the tax office just down the hall. She walked in, put her hand on my wife's arm, and said, "Chrissie, Mark's on the way to the hospital."

"No, no, no," Chris said as her colleague Samantha Pletscher and others tried to comfort her. "I went numb. People didn't know what to say," she remembered. "Complete disbelief. It was surreal. We were crying. People were at the service window looking in and seeing what was happening and saying 'Oh my God.' Everything was in a different realm."

Chris's main challenge was to get to Hartford Hospital. She called her sister, Mary Francini, who said she would drive. But by now, because of the crash, area roads were clogged with traffic rerouted from the Route 44 corridor. To circumvent the crowded roads, Chris's boss, Terry Colton, drove Chris to the Farmington Savings Bank parking lot in Unionville to rendezvous with Mary, who brought daughters Mikala and Rachel, ages 13 and 11. They would head south toward Plainville to hook up with Interstate 84 East into Hartford, thus avoiding local traffic.

"Please hurry, you have to get me there," Chris told Mary. At times like these, of course, every traffic light along the way was red. "It was the longest ride of my life," Chris said about the 15-mile drive. "Mary and the girls tried to keep me distracted." Rachel, who collected rubber wrist bands signifying various causes, pulled off her red band with the word "HOPE" (for finding a cure for multiple sclerosis) and gave it to Chris.

Among the people Chris called was Karen Wassell, one of my ING colleagues, to tell her that I was in the crash. "I had heard about the accident on the radio on my way into work," said Karen, who lives in Vernon, Conn. "I remember thinking, 'I hope Mark's okay.'" When she arrived at the ING building on Farmington Avenue in Hartford, Karen saw that I was not in my office. "I heard another report about this horrific accident, that it was very, very bad. There was a truck and cars were on fire. Then my phone rang and it was a number I didn't recognize on my caller ID. As soon as I heard Chris's voice, I asked, 'Oh my God, Chris, it's Mark and he's been in that accident?'"

When Chris arrived at the Hartford Hospital emergency room entrance, Karen was outside waiting for her. They hugged, and hospital volunteers escorted them to a nearby waiting room. At this point, they had no information about my condition, other than the fact that I had made it to the hospital. The worst thoughts filled the information void as they silently wondered if I was paralyzed, disfigured or dead. "A chaplain came into the room, and acknowledged the situation was bad," Karen said. "I kept hearing 'code red, code red.' I heard the helicopter. There were pamphlets in the room about death. Chris kept saying, 'Can you tell me how my husband is?' She was squeezing my hand so tight. They said a doctor is coming to talk to you. 'That's it,' I thought, 'he's coming in to tell us he's dead.'"

Within a few minutes, Dr. Gross walked in, shut the door and pulled up a chair. He saw the panicked look on Chris's face. "It's okay, he's alive," Dr. Gross said. He then explained my injuries – a punctured lung, broken arm, ribs, vertebrae, bruises and lacerations. "He's really banged up, but he's going to be okay," he said. "We're stabilizing him right now, then we'll move him up to the ICU [intensive care unit] where you'll be able to see him."

Chris and Karen made their way to the hospital's ICU waiting room on the 7th floor, where they were later joined by Mary, Mikala, Rachel and Chris's mom, Helen Silansky. The television in the waiting room carried frequent live bulletins from the scene of the crash. Chris saw my mangled car in front of the battered bus. Shortly after, one of Chris's best friends arrived at the emergency room. Cheryl Briere, then co-owner of the Hair Loft in Avon, had dropped everything after Chris called and drove straight to Hartford Hospital. After she arrived, not knowing yet that Chris had gone upstairs, Cheryl sat down in one of the ER waiting rooms.

"It was surreal," Cheryl remembered. "There was a lot of activity, but everyone was quiet, somber. At one point, I saw three guys wearing dark suits walk in, look around, then leave. It was eerie."

Just about everyone called Barbara Stotler "Bobbie." Then her son Chip and his wife Ellen had their first child, a baby girl they named Casey, who soon shortened her Grandma Bobbie's name by one syllable. Thus, Mrs. Barbara Stotler became "Bob."

Bobbie was not feeling well on that morning in late July. She had gone to a clinic for a blood test and returned to her Old Saybrook home. "I felt yucky," she said. "I walked in my room to lie down, and turned the TV on. I never turn it on during the day. I saw the accident on a news bulletin. I heard that if you had a relative who might have been involved that you can't contact, go to Hartford Hospital. I went running back out into my living room to look at my answering machine. Ellen had left a message. I called her and got her mother. She only knew that Chip had been in an accident, and that Ellen was on her way to Hartford Hospital."

Chip and Ellen were not the only members of the Stotler family who had been planning to leave on vacation the next day. Lorie McGarrahan, Chip's younger sister, was preparing her family to leave for Disney World in Florida. "I wanted to see what the weather was going to be so I turned on the TV," Lorie said. "I saw a report about the Avon crash. I saw a bus and flames and turned the TV off so my kids wouldn't see it. I thought, 'Chip's not at work today. He's going on vacation, too. Even so, I should call!' But everyone tells me that I worry about everything, so I didn't call. Then Ellen called me."

Lorie called her mom and they met in nearby Essex to drive the 50 miles to Hartford together. All they knew was that Chip was in the crash and that Ellen was on her way to the hospital. When they arrived at the emergency room entrance, she told a Hartford Hospital employee that her son had been in the Avon Mountain crash. "He looked at his computer, picked up a phone and turned his back on me and talked quietly on the phone," Bobbie said. "He didn't tell me anything except that they were sending someone down to walk to the room with me. I knew that this was not normal."

Hartford Courant.

America's Oldest Continuously Published Newspaper

WEATHER Chance Of Showers High Of 84. B6

SATURDAY, JULY 30, 2005   5★   Northwest Connecticut/Sports Final

AVON MOUNTAIN CRASH

THE TRUCK THAT CAUSED THE FIERY ACCIDENT AT THE BASE OF AVON MOUNTAIN FRIDAY
HAD A HISTORY OF CITATIONS FOR MECHANICAL PROBLEMS. ITS OWNER
HAS A RECORD OF SAFETY VIOLATIONS NEARLY THREE TIMES THE NATIONAL AVERAGE.

TRAGIC FAILURES

A POLICE officer works on the investigation of a fiery, deadly crash Friday on Route 44 at Route 10. The driver of a dump truck loaded with dirt and other debris lost control of his truck while heading down, crashing into eastbound cars and a bus stopped at a red light. Four people were killed, four were critically injured and 15 others were injured in the worst accident in the Hartford area in decades.

Four Dead, Nineteen Injured In Horrific Crash On Route 44

By DAVID OWENS, DANIEL P. JONES, And JESSE LEAVENWORTH
COURANT STAFF WRITERS

AVON — A loaded dump truck owned by a company with a long record of safety violations careened out of control Friday morning, causing a fiery crash at the base of Avon Mountain that killed four people and injured...

Doctor Springs To Action

A physician helped rescue victims at the scene and undoubtedly saved lives. Then, he went to work at the UConn Health Center. **Page A8**

Dump truck hits cars at intersection

See more detailed graphic, page A9

AVON

One Man's Commute To Emergency Room

By CAROLYN MOREAU
COURANT STAFF WRITER

Mark Robinson got up Friday morning, walked his dog and made a strawberry smoothie for his wife.

PLEASE SEE FOR ONE, PAGE A3

Photo by Shana Sureck

Hartford Courant, July 30, 2005

65

Avon rescuers on July 29, 2005 included (left to right) Fire Chief Jamie DiPace, Sue Kassey, Pete Delap and John Chevalier. They were among approximately 300 people who descended on the crash scene to help the victims of the crash.

Michael Cummings (center, white shirt) was seriously injured in the crash. He was rescued and cared for at the scene by Firefighter/Paramedics Victor Morrone and Tom Clynch, UConn Health Center Fire Department, Good Samaritan Lai Shawn Hooks and Dr. Scott Kurtzman.

West Hartford Detective Rob Magao (center) crawled into Chip Stotler's demolished car to comfort him as rescuers worked to free him. Farmington Fire Department Chief Tim Vibert (left) and Deputy Chief Jeff Hogan ultimately were able to get Chip out of the car and into the arms of the waiting LifeStar helicopter flight crew.

Ramona Juan Clark holds her wedding album with a photo of herself with her father, bus driver Frank Juan.

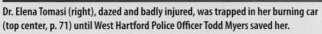
Dr. Elena Tomasi (right), dazed and badly injured, was trapped in her burning car (top center, p. 71) until West Hartford Police Officer Todd Myers saved her.

As part of its investigation, members of the elite North Central Municipal Accident Reconstruction Squad arranged 16 of the 19 vehicles involved in the crash in a field next to Towstar in Canton to help determine the sequence of events.

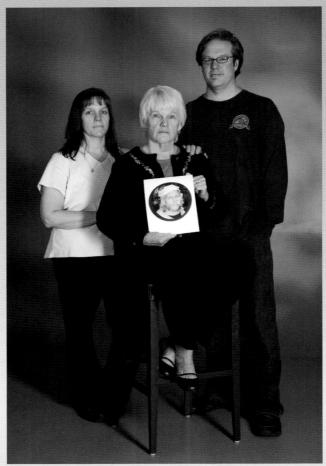

Bobbie Stotler (center) holds a photo of her son Chip. Standing with her are her daughter, Lorie McGarrahan, and her son, Johnny.

Chip Stotler's Gengras Center colleagues (left to right) Mike Gessford, Justin McGlamery, Peg Tompkins and John Drewry share their memories of Chip.

Members of the Gengras Center community (below), many wearing engineer's caps similar to the one Chip wore (right), offer a collective "bull moose" salute to Chip on the day they dedicated and named the playground he helped build the "Chip Stotler Adventure Education Area."

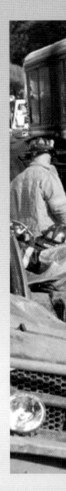

Kyle Caruso (left) was 21 years old and the maintenance manager at Avon Old Farms Hotel the day of the crash. He came running to my rescue, putting himself in harm's way in front of the still-running commuter bus, as he dug with his bare hands through the gravel that buried the seat belt release button. With the help of bus passenger Doug Smith, Kyle pulled me through the crushed driver's side window frame of my black Mercury Cougar.

Rescuers work feverishly to free Chip Stotler (top photo) whose car was just behind mine.

A slab of concrete had blasted through the windshield of my car, landing on the passenger-side seat.

Vincent Bongiovanni (center) holds the Bible he read with his mother, Barbara Bongiovanni, the night before she was killed in the Avon Mountain crash. Her brother, Floyd Amicone, holds a picture of his sister. Susan Dalgleish (right) was one of "Bongi's" beloved St. Francis Hospital colleagues.

Retired Hartford Police Detective LeRoy Pittman gave truck driver Raheem Naafi a ride to work the morning of the crash. His friend, Prenzina Holloway, rented a room to Raheem. "He told us the truck didn't have any brakes," Mrs. Holloway remembers. The cab of Truck 8 (below), where Raheem was trapped in the aftermath of the crash.

An aerial photo several hours after Truck 8 barreled down Avon Mountain
and crashed into 19 vehicles waiting at the traffic light.

Yvette Melling testified against her former boss, David Wilcox (below). The insurance fraud trial, which started in May 2008, ended in a mistrial. Juror Jon Warren (left) believed Mr. Wilcox was guilty, but could not convince three fellow jurors. Both Yvette and Jon were vindicated 10 months later when Mr. Wilcox pleaded no contest to insurance fraud, in addition to pleading guilty to four counts of manslaughter and five counts of assault.

The owner of American Crushing & Recycling, the company whose dump truck caused a fiery crash that killed four in Avon in July, agreed Monday to disclose all company and personal assets to a receiver and lawyers representing a man killed in the crash.

David R. Wilcox also agreed Monday to allow liens to be placed on all of his personal assets and company property.

Photo by Rick Hartford

Hartford Courant, October 18, 2005

'Guilty' On Nine Counts

AVON MOUNTAIN CRASH: Nearly Four Years Later, A Resolution For Survivors

Photo by Stephen Dunn

Hartford Courant, March 17, 2009

79

Dianna Hart Photography

Bride Tara Edlund Scott and her new husband Andrew gather with family at their wedding on July 11, 2009. Of her mom, Maureen, Tara said, "She was a wonderful, wonderful mother."

Oh! I have slipped the surly bonds of Earth

And danced the skies on laughter-silvered wings;

Sunward I've climbed and joined the tumbling mirth of sun-split clouds...

...Up, up the long, delirious, burning blue

I've topped the wind-swept heights with easy grace

Where never lark, nor even eagle, flew —

And, while with silent lifting mind I've trod

The high, untrespassed sanctity of space,

Put out my hand and touched the face of God.

John Gillespie Magee, Jr. (1922-1941);
born in Shanghai, China; pilot in Royal Canadian Air Force;
attended Avon Old Farms School, Avon, Connecticut.
Excerpted from Magee's 1941 poem "High Flight"

Cleanup crews still working after sunset, about 13 hours after the crash on July 29, 2005.

When they got to the room, Ellen was there. "She got up and hugged me and hugged me," Bobbie said. "I was hugging her back, and she was crying." There was another person in the room, a social worker. "I looked over Ellen's shoulder and asked if my son was dead. She said yes, she was really sorry. I couldn't believe it. I sat in a chair and just cried. Lorie came in then, and I told her. She sat and cried with us. It was just too horrible to comprehend."

Lorie's husband, John McGarrahan, called Bobbie's younger son, Johnny, with the terrible news. "He offered to come pick me up," Johnny said. "But I wasn't going to wait in Stamford while he drove to get me. I took the train home to New Haven, then drove to Hartford. It was really tough."

The Stotler women – Chip's wife, mother and sister – were asked if they wanted to see Chip. "We decided we needed to," Bobbie said. After all, could this possibly be true? Maybe it was a grotesquely cruel misunderstanding, a mistake, an unthinkable nightmare from which they would soon awake. How could the son, the husband, the brother, the father of five beautiful little girls, the beloved teacher, the man they loved so very much, the bright shining light in their lives and the lives of so many others, the most cheerfully positive and vibrant person they had even known...how could he, of all people, possibly be gone? And so Chip's wife, mother and sister braced themselves and walked together down a gloomy hospital corridor to see with their own eyes the utterly unimaginable.

Bus driver Frank Juan's daughter, Ramona, had 19 missed calls on her cell phone by the time she finally checked it in the early evening of July 29. It was only six weeks before her wedding, and she and her fiancé, Rick Clark, were vacationing in upstate New York in the Lake George region. "Mo, you gotta call home. Mo, you gotta call work," she said, recalling the recorded messages in her voicemail. "I finally called home and Alicia said, 'Granpa's been in a bad accident and they don't know if...' It took us only two hours to get back."

Within a tangle of beeping, flashing, pulsating wires, tubes and machines lay her heavily bandaged, sedated, comatose father, the man who was to walk her down the aisle in 43 days. But 65-year-old Frank Juan would not be going anywhere in 43 days. The man who always got the job done, the guy who averaged one sick day a decade, was on life support. A tracheal tube was inserted into his neck to keep the airway to his lungs open. A medical halo was surgically bolted directly to his head to keep it steady to prevent further damage from his broken neck and damaged spinal chord.

"I didn't think he was going to make it," Ramona said. "Someone told me that if I talked to him, he might be able to hear me. I just kept whispering in his ear, 'Dad, please don't go yet. You still have a job to do. Don't go yet, Dad, please don't go."

Bill Farrell desperately wanted someone to be with his niece, Tara Edlund, when he called with the devastating news. She had already lost her father when she was nine years old, and she had grown increasingly close to her mother, Maureen Edlund, in the 13 years since. Before calling Tara, Bill tried to contact Tara's boyfriend, Andrew Scott, who lived in Alexandria, Virginia. So did Tara, who had spent the day in a training class for her new position with the U.S. Department of Defense.

More than 135,000 people lived in Alexandria, just outside of Washington, D.C., and hundreds had the last name "Scott." Tara's uncle began frantically calling as many Scotts as he could, leaving messages to call him back if the last name "Edlund" sounded familiar. He eventually made contact with Andrew's parents.

"My dad called and said Tara's mother was in a bad accident, and they don't think she made it," Andrew said. His mom was the one who ultimately reached Tara at around 5 p.m. and told her she needed to call her Uncle Bill. Tara was with a few friends. They were planning to leave for a weekend in New York City.

"I called Uncle Bill and asked him to just tell me," Tara said. "I knew it had something to do with my mom. He told me there had been an accident, and that it was real bad. I said I already knew. He said, 'She's gone.'"

Tara's friends helped her walk a few blocks back to Union Station in Washington, within the shadow of the U.S. Capitol Building. They waited with her until Andrew's mother picked her up. By this time, managers at Maureen Edlund's employer, Jacobs Vehicle Systems, had already purchased plane tickets for Tara and Andrew for a 9:20 p.m. flight back to Connecticut.

"I was in complete shock," Tara said. "I was comatose. I didn't eat for two or three days. I was a zombie."

Retired Hartford Police Detective Leroy Pittman, the man who gave truck driver Raheem Naafi his last ride to work, heard about a big crash on Avon Mountain, and that it involved a truck. "I knew that Raheem was going to the mountain but, at first, I didn't give it a second thought," Det. Pittman said. "Until I was sitting there watching the news. And I saw this truck. And right away I thought about Raheem, and the brakes with this big load going down Avon Mountain. You can't stop. And then sure enough..."

Joseph "Frenchie" Cyr, another truck driver for American Crushing & Recycling, was waiting on the porch at 347 Sigourney Street in Hartford when Det. Pittman arrived there to see Raheem's landlord, Prenzina

Holloway, to talk about the crash. "He was there when I got there," Det. Pittman said. "He came to tell me about Raheem."

Two weeks later, Raheem's parents arrived at the house at 347 Sigourney Street. "Momma didn't say much," Mrs. Holloway said. "His dad asked me how I met Raheem. He wanted to know if he had been respectful."

Michael Cummings, the 35-year-old information technology supervisor at Saint Francis Hospital, never had a better reason for being late to work. Unlike the hundreds of previous commutes to his job in the Asylum Hill section of Hartford, however, instead of walking in through the employee entrance on Woodland Street, he would be entering the building flat on his back through the emergency room doors.

But Saint Francis was where Michael wanted to be. There had been some discussion at the accident scene about which hospital he should be sent to. During her phone call with Dr. Kurtzman, Tammy, Michael's wife, could hear him in the background screaming that he wanted to go to Saint Francis.

"I was coherent enough to know, I heard the helicopters landing, and I remember that I was relieved that I didn't have to go in the helicopter," Michael said. During the eight-mile ambulance ride to Saint Francis, as he worried about the possibility of being physically or mentally impaired, Michael did his own self assessment – wiggling his toes, remembering the alphabet, and counting toes and broken teeth.

"I picked a couple of pieces of teeth from my mouth because I broke four and cracked two," he said. "I don't know if that was from the airbag or when I bit down hard. My van was full of dirt, but I don't think I got hit by any rocks because I didn't have any major trauma to my face."

Meanwhile, "a million things" were going through the mind of Michael's wife, Tammy. She had pulled up to the front entrance of Saint Francis Hospital, and run inside to find out if Michael had been brought there. "They asked me who I was," she said. "They told me to go park. I asked them how he was, but they wouldn't say anything. I went back in, and they took me to a little back room in the Trauma area with a box of tissues, and I'm thinking, 'This isn't very good.'"

Beyond his physical condition, Michael remembers other concerns as he was brought into the Saint Francis emergency room. "We had just bought this new house and could barely afford it with both of us working full time," he said. "I remember thinking, 'Man, I hope I'm alright because I have a wife to support.' I was really worried."

As word of the crash spread throughout the halls of Saint Francis Hospital, Michael's IT colleagues would soon find out that, although seri-ously injured, he was going to survive. They were relieved. In the north wing of the hospital, about a thousand feet from the IT department, the women who worked in the business department would also learn that one of their colleagues was in the crash. There would be no sense of relief when they found out what happened to their beloved coworker and friend.

✧ ✧ ✧ ✧

The always-reliable Barbara Bongiovanni wasn't picking up her phone at her desk in the business department of Saint Francis Hospital. One of her Torrington neighbors had heard about the terrible crash in Avon. She called the hospital to check on her friend, to make sure she had arrived safely at work.

"I think she's in," said Sylvia Milner, Barbara's colleague, when the phone call rolled over to her line. Sylvia took the neighbor's name and number and said she would call back. "The strange thing was that I could have sworn I saw her come in that morning," Sylvia said. She walked over to Barbara's desk. It was ominously empty. There was no indication that she had arrived at work.

Another colleague, Susan Dalgleish, called Barbara's cell phone number. "There was absolutely no connection at all, no anything, not even her voicemail," Susan said. "I had a terrible feeling. And the girls kept saying, 'No, no, no, maybe she's just injured and can't get in touch with us.'"

They tried to carry on with their work while they waited for news, any news. It was nearly impossible. On a morning dominated by talk of a terrible disaster unfolding eight miles away, Bongi, their beloved colleague, was missing; no one knew where she was. A sense of dread descended upon the little family of ladies who worked in the business department of Saint Francis Hospital.

Later that day, they learned that Susan's worst fear turned out to be all too real. "Most of us worked with Bongi for 20 years or more," Sylvia said. "Every day, we see our co-workers more than we see our family. She was part of our family. I had never experienced a death so tragic. It was the worst day of my life."

✧ ✧ ✧ ✧

Saint Francis would receive one other crash victim that morning, someone who was not an employee. Dr. Elena Tomasi, the dentist from Belarus who was dramatically rescued from her burning car with only moments to spare, remembers the emergency medical people talking to her as they prepared her for the ambulance ride to the hospital.

"I heard parts of sentences and people talking," Elena said. "They repeatedly asked me questions like, 'Where are you?' They told me there was an accident in Avon. They asked me what happened. They asked who was with me in the car. I immediately thought of Vlad [her 13-year-old son]. I had such a bad feeling, like I was the only survivor. Why did they ask me who was with me in the car?"

Minutes earlier she had been lying on the lawn of Nassau's furniture story, covered in blood from a bad head wound. Her face swelled. Bus passenger Ed Giarnese held Elena's head while Avon Police Officer Sue Kassey removed a piece of glass from her left eye.

"I started blinking," Elena said. "I was in and out of consciousness." She also remembered a doctor who treated her at the scene. "He was an endocrinologist. I remember his face. I wanted to thank him for helping me." Like many good Samaritans on this tragic day, the unidentified doctor did what he could to help and then quietly left the scene before anyone could thank him.

During her ambulance ride to the hospital, as she worried about her son and husband, Dr. Tomasi finally remembered that she had been in her car alone because she was going to work. That realization brought her a sense of relief. But she was still bewildered and, on this warm sunny morning, she was cold. "I started to feel the chills," she said. People were telling her not to fall asleep. "Oh my God, I am very serious," she thought. "If I fall asleep, I will probably never wake up and I will never forgive myself. Just stay awake. I felt so tired. I really, really wanted to fall asleep, but I was saying to myself, 'Just do not close your eyes.' I was forcing myself to stay awake."

Lai Shawn Hooks, the medical assistant who was on her way to her job at the Avon Medical Group when she came upon the crash, had already called Orlando Tomasi, Elena's husband. Of the many good Samaritans who stopped to help, Lai Shawn took a particularly active role. It wasn't easy. When she initially arrived at the intersection, traveling west down Avon Mountain, traffic was already backed up. The crash had just happened. The wheels on the overturned dump truck were still spinning. In a moment of horror, as the truck burst into flames, Lai Shawn got out of her car to witness the unbelievable spectacle. A guy in a car behind her started honking his horn. Where exactly was he going to go at that horrific moment – as people were dying right before his eyes – in a line of backed-up, bumper-to-bumper traffic?

Lai Shawn knew what she had to do. "All I was thinking was, 'What can I do?'" she said. "People were in need right there. Why would I go this way or that way and say it's not my business? Someone's dying. Why would you not park your damn car and get over there and help?" Among the many forms of help Lai Shawn provided that morning, she took it upon herself to contact as many of the victims' families as she could.

After Lai Shawn's call to Elena's husband, a doctor at Saint Francis called Elena's son, Vlad. "I told the doctor to please tell him that I was okay. I didn't want him to worry."

Then Elena was taken to have a CAT scan done, an X-ray procedure that produces cross-sectional pictures of the body. "While they were taking me there, all of a sudden, flashes of memory came back," Elena said. "I remembered what happened. I remembered the very last moment before I lost consciousness. The truck hit me."

CHAPTER 10

"Highway of Death"

Avon Town Manager Phil Schenck had passed through the intersection only minutes before the crash on his way to a Rotary Club meeting at Avon Old Farms Hotel. "I arrived at the hotel and paid for my breakfast," he said. "Then I heard sirens. Chief Agnesi came in and said we had a serious accident out there. I walked out and saw a plume of smoke."

His first reaction was to consult with Chiefs DiPace and Agnesi, to make sure they had what they needed. At one point he stood on the knoll near Nassau's furniture store to survey the scene. Mr. Schenck, a retired U.S. Army lieutenant colonel who served in Operation Desert Storm, was immediately reminded of something he had seen in February 1991. "It looked like the 'Highway of Death,'" he said, recalling the notorious, heavily bombed road between Kuwait City and Basra, Iraq. "It was carnage."

The trail of mangled vehicles and broken bodies extended about 100 yards, from the intersection at the base of Avon Mountain to where the overturned truck ground to a halt and burned. Into this valley of hurt came an army of everyday people – professional and volunteer emergency services workers and Good Samaritans – people who made humanity their business on this tragic day.

After taking care of the immediate crises of burning vehicles and critically injured motorists, the rescuers still had much to do. Truck 8's path of destruction stretched out before them; the acrid odor of burned rubber and fuel still hung heavily in the air.

Truck 8's journey was over, but the long process of determining the cause of the crash was just beginning. It was crucial to gather the clues that would help answer the questions of how and, maybe, why. However, about an hour after Truck 8 delivered its devastating blow, rescuers were thinking about a more immediate, gut-wrenching duty. Weighing heavily on their hearts and minds was the need to carefully remove the deceased.

"People were traumatized by the devastation of the crash," said Dan Jones, the Hartford Courant reporter. "Most people there were just doing their work – emergency people, press people, whoever – but they had this look of shock on their faces. There was a certain solemnity to what was going on. There was a different mood about the place because it was so horrific."

Emergency services workers – police, fire, medical – have a culture of toughness driven by the necessity of dealing with highly stressful, physically and emotionally demanding situations. But in the end, to echo Shakespeare, "If you prick them they will bleed." They are, after all, human; even helpers need help.

Jamie DiPace, chief of the Avon Volunteer Fire Department, understood this. By state statute, as the senior ranking fire officer, he had ultimate responsibility for the overall crash scene. Among his concerns was the psychic toll the crash would take on rescuers. He wanted the Connecticut Critical Incident Team there as soon as possible.

"The public assumes that because emergency services workers deal with traumatic events day in and day out that they're not bothered by them," said Charles Epstein, operational director of the team, and court planner for Judicial Marshal Services for Connecticut Superior Court Operations. "Nothing could be further from the truth. They are caring human beings. That's why they've chosen these professions."

The Critical Incident Team has 60 members statewide, all with experience as emergency services workers. Their mission is to provide emergency crisis support for police, fire and emergency medical workers. Like so many of the people who responded to the Avon Mountain accident, Marshal Epstein's service on the Team was purely volunteer, provided on his own time. When the request for the Team's services came in, he received permission to leave his day-time job in Hartford.

"I was just totally amazed by what I saw," Marshal Epstein said, remembering his first impression of the crash scene. "I'd been in the emergency services business for 37 years. I've been at plane crashes, bus accidents, motor vehicle crashes. I have never seen anything that spread out, that devastating, that number of mangled, burned vehicles, with sand and dirt and gravel all over the place. It was eye-popping, devastating."

Tents with food, water and chairs for the rescuers were set up on the lawn of Nassau's furniture store. An emergency services communications bus from Newington was nearby. Avon Town Manager Phil Schenck told Chief DiPace that he could count on whatever support he felt was necessary.

"Phil was very reassuring," Chief DiPace said. "You can't ask for any better. People just appeared to help us. People from Avon Old Farms Inn gave us food and water and access to restrooms. A woman came down from her home on Vermillion Road and handed out water for six hours at the rehab tent. Lai Shawn Hooks was there helping everyone all day. You can't ask for better support than we received that day."

Valerie Sedor, five months pregnant and late for work due to backed-up traffic, arrived at her job at Avon Old Farms Inn at around 8:30 a.m. She knew about the crash because both of her sisters had already called to check on her. Joanne Fenn, an accountant at the Inn, was waiting for her. Together they began bringing out cases of bottled water to the rescuers.

"What do you need? What can we do?" Valerie asked. "We just did whatever we could to help." Throughout the day, Valerie, Joanne and the Avon Old Farms Inn staff provided anything they could for the rescuers, including use of the inn itself for its meeting room and restroom facilities.

Ann Ryan, a member of the Avon Fire Department Ladies Auxiliary, called her husband, Asst. Chief Delap, to find out what she should bring to the scene. "What do you need?" she asked. "They said, 'Bring water.' So I dragged it over just as one of the LifeStar helicopters was taking off. Everybody can do their part in some way."

After the wounded were removed and transported to local hospitals, Chief DiPace brought all the first responders over toward the rehab tent. "I sat them down and talked to them," he said. "I told them they did a great job. This was about two hours after the crash occurred. The extrication of the victims still in their cars hadn't taken place yet. I asked for volunteers to help remove the bodies. Several people stepped up. We had the stress team there when we did the extrications."

The Rev. Jon Widing, the Avon Police chaplain, was also there, supporting the rescuers and performing last rites for Maureen Edlund, Barbara Bongiovanni and Abdulraheem Naafi. Dr. Wayne Carver, the Connecticut chief medical examiner, arrived to officially declare them dead. With orange tarp in place to provide privacy, their bodies were removed and taken to the medical examiner's office in nearby Farmington. Among its responsibilities was to determine the cause of death and to "identify, document and interpret relevant forensic scientific information for use in criminal and civil legal proceedings necessary in the investigation of violent, suspicious and sudden unexpected deaths."[1]

That the deaths of Maureen Edlund, Barbara Bongiovanni, Raheem Naafi and Chip Stotler were unexpected, sudden and violent was obvious. Whether they were suspicious – the result, for example, of someone's wrongdoing and/or negligence, acts of commission or omission – would be the focus of a massive investigation that began as soon as Capt. Rinaldo started roping off the mountain to protect potential evidence.

"I wanted to make sure we had enough resources, and to coordinate what was going on," he said. Within minutes of the massive collision, approximately 300 emergency services workers were on the scene. "We had to maintain control," Capt. Rinaldo said, which involved shutting down the mountain to traffic and bringing in forensic teams to protect anything that may eventually be needed as evidence for the crash investigation.

That investigation would be handled by the North Central Municipal Accident Reconstruction Squad (NCMARS), the regional team that investigates serious crashes in nine Hartford County towns, including Avon.

"The regional accident reconstruction team is the best in the state

1. www.ct.gov/ocme/site/default.asp

and maybe even the country," Capt. Rinaldo said. "The evidence trail was outstanding, one of the best I've ever seen. The evidence-collection procedures were almost perfect." If this crash led to a criminal case, Capt. Rinaldo wanted to be sure that the investigation phase was handled as professionally and thoroughly as possible. "I wanted to make sure there would be no holes in the case," he said.

✧ ✧ ✧ ✧

Avon Police Officer John Chevalier was planning on sleeping a little later than usual on this Friday morning. He had been putting in long hours investigating a fatal crash that had taken place two weeks earlier on Avon Mountain.

"Karen, my wife, woke me and said there was a bad crash," he said. "I turned on my radio and heard there was a truck on fire. Then my pager went off." He rushed off from his New Hartford home to the Avon Police Department, about a mile from the crash site. "It was a ghost town," he said. "There was only one vehicle left in the back of the building. I had never seen that before in my 18 years with the department. I got in the Expedition, and headed to the crash."

In addition to his regular responsibilities, Officer Chevalier, 44 years old, was a member of the regional accident investigation team. After helping out with various aspects of the immediate after-crash activities, Officer Chevalier began to deal with some of his accident-investigation responsibilities. At around noon, Avon Police Sergeant Gerald Post asked for his help.

"This is Mr. Wilcox," Sgt. Post told Officer Chevalier. "He owns the truck. Can you take him inside and take a statement from him?" The accident reconstruction squad's command trailer was a large motor coach, which was set up in Nassau's parking lot near the Soccer Unlimited store. At this point, the bodies had not yet been removed.

"We went inside the command trailer and started talking," Officer Chevalier said. "Then Mr. Wilcox slid a piece of paper over toward me. He didn't really say anything. I said, 'Is this for me?' And he said yes. I looked down, and it was a photocopy of an insurance identification card. It had '#8' written on the side."

Connecticut law requires that vehicles operating on public highways maintain liability insurance. If you canceled that insurance, you would be contacted by the Department of Motor Vehicles (DMV) reminding you that Connecticut law requires liability insurance. Unless you had a commercial policy, that is. In that case, you would not be contacted because every single member of the 1993 Connecticut legislature voted to give a special exclusion to commercial entities.

Even so, the vast majority of business owners operating commercial vehicles did carry liability insurance because of the obvious danger and risk to property and innocent people inherent in the operation of any motor vehicle, especially large trucks. "No good businessman in this world goes without insurance," said Jack Matava, owner of Edward Motor Service in Unionville, Conn. "I would never think of taking one of my tow trucks out without insurance on it, or sending one of my guys out. You know what? All the money in the world...it's not worth it."

"I just put his photocopy of the insurance card aside at the time," said Officer Chevalier. "Part of the norm in accidents involving trucks was that they would make copies of their insurance cards and give them to us later. So it was unusual for someone to volunteer an insurance document in the immediate aftermath of a crash."

At that moment, Officer Chevalier had no way of knowing the photocopy of the insurance card represented a policy that had been canceled by ACR more than six months earlier. Was that simply an oversight on Wilcox's part? Between 7:53 a.m. that morning, 15 minutes after the crash, and 8:39 a.m., there were at least a dozen calls between David and Donna Wilcox. Donna Wilcox had been on the phone several times with Webster Insurance, first to check the status of ACR trucks' liability insurance, and then to try to retroactively reinstate liability coverage. That was necessary because ACR had canceled liability insurance on its fleet of 12 dump trucks, including Truck 8, back on Jan. 3, 2005.

As Officer Chevalier finished taking a statement from Mr. Wilcox, he told him to raise his right hand and asked, "Are the contents of this statement true and correct to the best of your knowledge?" Mr. Wilcox answered, "Yes."

CHAPTER 11

A Deadly Loophole

Laws are like sausages. It is better not to see them being made.[1]

— Otto von Bismarck

Well before there was any hint of fraud, there was the Connecticut State Legislature and Public Act 93-298—sHB 5435: An Act Concerning Cancelation and Nonrenewal of Automobile Insurance Coverages.

The legislation was intended to get uninsured motorists off the road, which is a very good idea given that the cost of covering the irresponsible is ultimately borne by those who play by the rules. But the legislation excluded commercial vehicles. Why? And what if commercial vehicles had not been excluded? Would David Wilcox's wretchedly maintained Truck 8 have been barreling down Avon Mountain the morning of July 29, 2005 if the insurance reform law approved in 1993 by all 187 members of Connecticut's House and Senate had applied to all motor vehicles and not just private-passenger automobiles?

Again, the intent of the 1993 legislation was good. As stated in a June 5, 1993 *Hartford Courant* article, "In an effort to keep uninsured motorists off the road, the House of Representatives approved legislation Friday that would require insurers to notify the state every time an automobile policy is canceled. The legislation, which was co-sponsored by all 151 members of the House, would allow motor vehicle officials to know for the first time when motorists drop insurance coverage that is required by law. The commissioner of motor vehicles would be required to cancel the registration of any vehicle for which the insurance lapses, and authorities would be able to confiscate the license plates...the insurance industry supports the legislation, but its representatives said more than the legislation is necessary to get uninsured drivers – whose accidents drive up the cost of insurance – off the road.

"What it really comes down to is enforcement," said John Miletti, a lobbyist with the Insurance Association of Connecticut. Connecticut law requires drivers to carry a card that is proof of their insurance, but some drivers stop payment on their policies after getting the card. Currently there is no way for motor vehicle officials and police to quickly know when a card is not valid. The bill passed Friday would create a registry that police could consult when they stop a motorist for any motor vehicle violation."[1]

---

1. *Hartford Courant*, June 5, 1993, p. A7, "Bill Passes Requiring that State Know When Car Insurance Lapses"

If there was a registry, police would have been able to check it on July 29, 2005, when David Wilcox volunteered an insurance card for a policy that was canceled seven months earlier. Even better – immeasurably better – had the 1993 legislation included commercial vehicles, chances are that the authorities may have been able to take action against ACR and its uninsured fleet before people died.

So again, the question: Why did the 1993 Connecticut State Legislature unanimously vote to explicitly exclude commercial vehicles?

"There is no rational or defensible policy explanation for not requiring truck companies to meet the same standards," said Connecticut Attorney General Richard Blumenthal after the Avon Mountain crash.[2]

"It seems to me like a major loophole that ought to be fixed," said Michael Riley, president of the Motor Transport Association of Connecticut.[3] "It's not something we would take up as a cause to exempt trucks from insurance reporting," he said of his 1,000-member association.

But there it was, in Section 38a-343a of The General Statutes of Connecticut. While insurance companies that issued "private passenger motor vehicle liability insurance policies in this state shall...notify the Commissioner of Motor Vehicles of the cancelation by the insurance company of all such policies which occurred during the preceding month... *no such notification shall be made for any cancelation of any policy of commercial insurance.*" (Author's italics.)

Members of the 1993 Connecticut legislature appeared to be oblivious to the potential consequences of that exception. Indeed, if anything, there was much self-congratulatory backslapping taking place upon voting the proposal into law.

Kevin Sullivan, a future lieutenant governor and, at the time, a state senator representing West Hartford, said, "I rise to commend, in particular, Senator Williams and the entire committee [for] bringing forward a bill that addresses concerns that I think each of us hear quite often from our constituents with respect to the need to find a system that works as opposed to the [one] that's in place right now."[4]

So: Who asked for the exclusion? Why? And why was it granted? I asked several members of that 1993 legislature who voted for it.

A friend of mine, Patrick Flaherty, was a freshman state representative for the 8th District in eastern Connecticut in 1993, covering Coventry, Columbia and parts of Lebanon and Vernon. I had met him at Second Congregational Church in Coventry, where we both served in various volunteer roles. We also became acquainted through our involvement with

---

2. *Hartford Courant*, Sept. 24, 2005, p. A12, "Widow Sues Dump Truck Owner in Avon Crash; State Also Put on Notice Over Route 44 Safety"

3. same as above

4. Connecticut General Assembly, Senate Proceedings 1993, Vol. XX, p. 4467.

town government. I was elected to Coventry's Board of Education in 1993. By that time, even though he's five years younger than I, Patrick had already served terms as chairman of both the town council and board of education.

"I was a legislator for 10 years, I'm working on a Ph.D in economics from UConn, and I still can't figure out auto insurance," said Patrick in a 2008 interview. He also has an undergraduate degree from Harvard. "The 1993 session was the first after the state income tax was instituted. Emotions were still raw; there was a lot of angst. I remember that we were looking for ways to give taxpayers a break. We were focused on getting uninsured motorists off the roads, which would lower insurance premiums for everyone."

As a freshman legislator in 1993, Patrick readily admits that he was naïve to the mechanisms of state government. "It was a heavily lobbied bill. I went on the faith of people I trusted. They told me it was a good bill. I should have known more about it before I voted for it."

Is it possible that the exclusion for commercial insurance policies was somehow inadvertent? Not likely, Patrick said. "Believe me, people who had a stake in it knew every single comma in [the bill's language]. Somebody always knew what was going on. Honest mistakes happen, but I doubt that this was one of them."

It's entirely possible that the exclusion was, perhaps, what it appears to be: an attempt by some legislators to look out for what they perceived to be the legitimate interests of the construction industry during tough economic times.

"Of course, even if the motivation was well-meaning, it was still a policy error – one that had tragic consequences," Patrick said. "And it was an error that might have been prevented if this provision had received greater scrutiny and attention in a public hearing or in debate on the floor of the House or Senate."

Donald E. Williams, Jr., is a nine-term state senator representing the 29th District in eastern Connecticut. He was first elected in 1993, and is currently also President Pro Tempore, the highest-ranking legislator in the Connecticut legislature. "I do not have a specific recollection of the legislative history of this statute," he wrote in response to a letter I had sent him.

Sen. Williams asked an aide to contact the Office of Legislative Research. Among other things, the OLR research report said, "It is unclear why this exemption was included...There was nothing contained in the transcript of the public hearing relating to this bill that dealt with this issue...the exemption was not addressed in either the Senate or House debate on the amended bill."

Attorney Kevin Rennie, retired state representative (1989-1995) and senator, who now writes a Sunday column for the *Hartford Courant*, wrote, "What I recall most vividly was that nearly every member of the House of Representatives (I was one of them) co-sponsored that bill. There was something that caused that bill not only to fly through the legislature but to capture the attention of so many legislators. I can only speculate, but there must have been something in the news that year that prompted everyone to jump on the bill. I shudder at how that commercial exemption made its way into it."

Louis C. DeLuca, retired state senator and ranking member of the 1993 senate insurance committee, wrote: "The exclusion for commercial vehicles was presented by the construction industry. They register their fleets but the nature of the business is such that all vehicles are not in use at the same time. The insurance policies require [the insured] to advise the insurance companies which vehicles are on the road or job. They may have 12 trucks, as an example, but only four or five on the only job they have going. The system works except for those who try to beat it, like in [the Avon Mountain crash] situation. As far as I know, there have been very few violations because, as in this case, they could lose everything.... This is not the first time he [David Wilcox] did this, but the first time he got caught."

I called the government relations department of the Connecticut Construction Industries Association (CCIA), which represents Connecticut's commercial construction industry. A spokesman told me that he researched the issue but was not able to find any records linking CCIA with the legislative exclusion for commercial insurance.

I called James Amann several times. He was elected as a state representative in 1990 and served as Speaker of the House from 2005 to 2008 when he retired to focus on running for governor. He didn't return my calls. I went to his campaign web site called "Jim Amann for Governor 2010 – All Voices Heard," and wrote a letter asking him to comment. No response. So much for his campaign slogan.

On June 26, 2009, I sent a note to Governor M. Jodi Rell, who was elected in 1985 as state representative for the 107th District in Brookfield, and was one of the legislators who voted to approve the statute that included the exclusion loophole for commercial entities. Here's the note I received in response to my letter:

Dear Mr. Robinson,

Thank you for your email to Governor Rell requesting an interview with her for your book on the Avon Mountain Crash before July 10th. Unfortunately, we are not able to schedule an interview at this time. The Governor's schedule is unusually busy with the current state budget deficit. Thank you for your understanding.

Best regards,
Elaina
Elaina Parahus

Scheduler
Office of Governor M. Jodi Rell

The loophole was acknowledged and closed two months after the July 29, 2005 crash with the passage of Emergency Certified S.B. 2102, LCO 8489, An Act Strengthening Enforcement of Mandatory Security Requirements For Motor Vehicles With A Commercial Registration. On Oct. 26, 2005, State Senator Joseph J. Crisco said, "...this addresses the concerns of the people of Connecticut and, in particular, this august body, from that horrible day in July when on Avon Mountain a truck went out of control and created havoc among those on the road, resulting in several deaths and also a considerable amount of injury, and unbelievable harm at the present time and in the future, particularly for the victims and the victims' families."[5]

As a result of the new law, any commercial vehicle owner who knowingly operates or permits the operation of a vehicle without insurance would be guilty of a Class D felony, and would face up to five years in prison or a fine of $5,000, or both.

That's a step in the right direction, although the proposed fine of $5,000 is insultingly small considering the potential consequences. And, for that matter, it's virtually no deterrent for the David Wilcoxes of the world – those who would try to save a few bucks by canceling their liability insurance at the expense of potential crash victims. A possible $5,000 fine is still much less expensive than keeping a fleet of large trucks properly insured.

And finally, for the victims of the Avon Mountain crash, the new legislation was the proverbial "day late and dollar short," to say the very least.

5. S-523, Connecticut Gen. Assembly, Senate, Proceedings 2005, Special Sessions, Vol. 48, Part 20, p. 6226.

CHAPTER 12

The CSI of Crash Analysis

A nother day and another fully loaded Mack dump truck flies down Avon Mountain heading straight for the intersection of Nod Road and Routes 10 and 44. It was September 11, 2006. The driver's heart pounds as, once again, the canopy of trees morphs into a green blur as the truck picks up speed...50 miles an hour...60...70... then he hit the brakes...and the truck skids to a stop.

He turned around and did it again, driving down the mountain once more with the truck fully loaded – and again the truck stopped when he hit the brakes. And then one more time, fully loaded, and it stopped again. Then he did it three times with an empty truck. It stopped each time.

Sitting beside him in the passenger seat on those trips down the mountain that early morning was Suffield Police Capt. David Bourque, the head of the North Central Municipal Accident Reconstruction Squad (NCMARS), which investigates serious motor vehicle collisions. It is one of several regional law-enforcement teams in Connecticut that share resources. The team comprises 14 members from nine towns: Avon, Bloomfield, Canton, Farmington, Granby, Simsbury, Suffield, Windsor and Windsor Locks. The regional approach gives each town access to skilled people and equipment that local police often cannot afford to supply on their own.

"Let me tell you, coming down that mountain, I thought we were going to flip," Capt. Bourque said. "I remember thinking, 'why are we doing this?' and 'was this still a good idea?' and 'I hope we can stop this thing.'"

One worry he did not have was other vehicles getting in the way. At 4 o'clock that morning, the NCMARS team shut down the mountain and closed off the intersection to conduct the test. Inspectors from the Commercial Vehicle Safety Division of the Department of Motor Vehicles (DMV) were on hand to examine the truck ahead of time and after each test. They verified that it had properly functioning brakes.

"As the inspectors said, this is what the dump truck was designed to do, stop and load, haul and go, if properly maintained. We proved that a Mack dump truck, loaded or empty, will stop when its brakes are working correctly," Capt. Bourque said, noting that they relied only on the brakes that morning, not downshifting or the Jake Brake engine retarder to slow or stop the truck.

That fact might have presented a problem for David Wilcox and his lawyers. After all, if they were going to blame the entire fiasco on the alleged incompetence of Truck 8's driver, Abdulraheem Naafi, who was conveniently dead and therefore unable to defend himself, how would they explain the results of the September 11, 2006 test? If the case went to trial, perhaps they could convince at least one gullible juror that maybe Raheem didn't shift properly and that was why the truck crashed. But what would they say about the brakes? As the test proved, Mack dump trucks with properly functioning brakes stop when the driver hits the brake pedal, whether the truck is empty or fully loaded, whether it's going 10 miles an hour or 70, whether it's on a level surface or steep downgrade. It doesn't matter what Raheem may or may not have been doing with the clutch and transmission as Truck 8 flew down the mountain. Are we to believe that he never tried the brakes? Please. And prior to arriving at the top of Avon Mountain, between the ACR lot in Bloomfield and Deercliff Road, his intended destination, there were no long downslopes on which Raheem could have overheated the brakes, which would reduce their effectiveness. So Mr. Wilcox would need to explain the inexplicable: Why didn't Truck 8 stop when Raheem hit the brakes?

That would not be the only problem for a Wilcox trial defense. The NCMARS squad had a conviction rate of 100 percent for the cases it investigated, which included all the cases in which defendants decided to cop a plea rather than face the science and professionalism of NCMARS. "We're like the CSI [Crime Scene Investigation] TV show," Capt. Bourque said, "except that our focus is on analyzing crash scenes."

In the investigation of the July 29, 2005 Avon Mountain crash, the NCMARS team assembled a final report well over a thousand pages long. The warrant for Wilcox's eventual arrest would provide a summary of that report, from the results of sophisticated laboratory tests to what investigators saw with their own eyes at the horrific crash scene.

Windsor Police Officer Russ Wininger, a team leader and member of NCMARS since 1996 (and now a detective), was home packing for a vacation when he received a voicemail about the crash. As he raced to the scene, he saw the column of smoke. "It was overwhelming," he said, remembering his first impression when he arrived at the scene of the crash. "It was the biggest crash site I had ever seen."

In addition to the obvious devastation just past the intersection, truck parts littered the mountain starting near Wright Drive, which is about 2,600 feet – or almost nine football fields – from the intersection. One of Officer Wininger's primary responsibilities that day was to walk the crash scene and find physical evidence.

"I remember walking up the mountain and thinking, 'What happened?'" he said. "There was a tidal wave of debris. Something catastrophic happened to that truck before it crashed. There were parts all over the place. I'd never seen anything like that before. If those pieces were there on the mountain, that obviously meant they were not functioning in the truck."

Officer Wininger knew the physical evidence would play a crucial role in the inevitable litigation that would follow an event of this magnitude. "It was one of the biggest crashes any of us would encounter in our careers," he said. "There was no rush. We had to get it right. Most crashes are the result of exceeding the capability of the driver, the vehicle or the roadway. We knew that no one at the bottom of the mountain was responsible for this crash, so it was a matter of documenting the other three."

Capt. Bourque, with his engineering and surveying background, had brought a higher level of sophistication to the team's investigatory capabilities. One example was the use of the "Total Station" prism-and-pole tool, a laser measuring system that provides a three-dimensional perspective. It is typically used by civil engineers and land surveyors to measure not only precise distances but topography, thus creating a visual dimension of the mountain and crime scene.

"Many law enforcement people are drawn to what some consider 'more glamorous' jobs, like SWAT [special weapons and tactics], narcotics or the K-9 unit," Officer Wininger said. "The people on the NCMARS team are a different breed. We really like what we're doing. Some people try to get involved without realizing how much math and science is required. That's when they discover that maybe this type of work is not for them."

The NCMARS team located and identified 614 points of evidence that day, everything from clutch and transmission parts to "tire shadow" skid marks and gouges from the truck's lug nuts grinding into the asphalt after it flipped. And then there were the pieces of the pressure plate, the steel, heavy-duty, half-inch-thick part of the transmission assembly that pushes the clutch disc against the engine flywheel.

"The pressure plate blew apart; I've never seen that before in my career," said Chip Mowrey, the service manager at Gabrielli Truck Sales in Hartford, who has been involved with truck repairs for several decades. As service manager, he was supervisor of 11 mechanics who maintain and repair large trucks. "When that disintegrated, when the pressure plate came apart, being that the air lines and everything else are right there, it's going to take out quite a few [other parts]. That had to be a significant event when that thing blew apart."

That disintegration may have been related to Truck 8's previously repaired clutch plate, which the NCMARS investigation determined was wobbling because the pilot bearing designed to steady it for proper shifting had apparently never been reinstalled. The shards of the broken pressure plate were found near Wright Drive, which is seven-tenths of a mile after Deercliff Road, where Raheem was supposed to turn left. For reasons no one will ever know for sure, he missed that turn and started the gradual descent down Avon Mountain. He had plenty of time to start hitting the brakes well before reaching the steep downhill grades prior to Wright Drive. He had to be desperate by the time he reached Wright Drive and the final steep downgrade before the intersection of Nod Road and Routes 10 and 44.

Regarding those brakes, the investigation found – among a total of 20 pre-crash equipment violations – mismatched brake chambers, misadjusted brakes, oversized brake drums, contaminated brake linings, a defective brake slack adjuster and an inoperative parking brake. In summary, according to DMV Inspector Paul Pelletier, Truck 8's "remaining stopping power was not enough to overcome the momentum and force of the loaded vehicle."[1]

NCMARS also brought in Scott Corbett, an expert with Haldex Brake Products, a leading global supplier of heavy-duty air brakes and other parts, to assist with the inspection of Truck 8, which had Haldex parts. He examined Truck 8's brakes and reported that "the accident vehicle was poorly maintained, and the brakes were improperly adjusted on multiple occasions. The brake components demonstrated that industry standard and manufacturer's recommended maintenance did not take place on this truck, creating suboptimal operation conditions. The maintenance methods employed would have led to additional brake failures."[2]

In other words, the brakes on Truck 8 "sucked," as described by John Antoniak, David Wilcox's stepson.[3]

It was the NCMARS investigation that led to Mr. Wilcox's arrest a year after the crash. "David and Shaun Wilcox rooted around [Truck 8] late into the night last July 28, hours before the vehicle would become a killing machine," wrote Dan Jones and Katie Melone in a July 25, 2006 *Hartford Courant* article.[4] "The dump truck was falling apart – specifically its brakes, as two previous drivers had repeatedly warned – and the father and son were trying to get the 2000 Mack back on the road for a delivery on Avon Mountain the next morning. As usual with [Truck 8] – according to a 38-page arrest affidavit – David Wilcox was doing things on the cheap. It was a pattern that was evident for years at his Bloomfield trucking companies, the affidavit says. The drivers' entreaties for full repairs were ignored; the brakes were never fixed. Wilcox himself loaded the truck the next morning with tons of construction debris and sent this newly hired driver on his way to the mountain, the affidavit says."

The investigation also determined that the newly hired driver, Abdulraheem Naafi, had never undergone "pre-employment controlled

1. Arrest warrant affidavit, CFS#: 0500016324, p. 14, #25.
2. Arrest warrant affidavit, CFS#: 0500016324, p. 15, #26.
3. Arrest warrant affidavit, CFS#: 0500016324, p. 29, #46.
4. *Hartford Courant*, July 25, 2006, "Conscious, Reckless Behavior," by Daniel P. Jones and Katie Melone

substance testing," which was not uncommon among ACR drivers. The investigation revealed that several ACR drivers had not been tested. According to at least one industry expert, missing that test is more than just an oversight or violation of the law.

"That's a mortal sin," said Mike Riley, president of the Motor Transport Association of Connecticut for 23 years. "You don't put a guy into your truck without doing a pre-employment drug test. It's basic. You're taking a big chance, putting a guy in there without knowing if he's clean."

Flouting the law apparently was just business as usual for David Wilcox, as chronicled throughout the NCMARS final report. It all added up to "a pattern of non-compliance with State and Federal requirements, specifically for controlled substance testing, driver qualification, files, maintenance records and vehicle maintenance."[5] According to the arrest affidavit, "This conscious and reckless behavior caused the death of four persons identified as Maureen Edlund, Barbara Bongiovanni, Paul (Chip) Stotler and Abdul Raheem Naafi. These deaths constitute four counts of Manslaughter in the First Degree...This conscious and reckless behavior caused the serious physical injury of Elena Tomasi, Frank Juan, Jr., Mark Robinson, Michael Cummings and Iris Rich. These injuries constitute five counts of Assault in the First Degree."[6]

---

5. Arrest warrant affidavit, CFS#: 0500016324, p. 34, #53.
6. Arrest warrant affidavit, CFS#: 0500016324, p. 35, #54.

CHAPTER 13

"It Was So Hard"

The Juan family home is in an old, Polish neighborhood in Torrington, sitting up on a knoll between a red-brick factory on one side and St. Mary's Church on the other. On the morning of July 29, 2005, when 65-year-old Frank Juan left the blue, vinyl-sided, two-story house – the one he and his wife, Ann, bought 14 years ago to raise their children – he had no way of knowing how much would be gone by the time he returned. For starters, he would miss his own birthday and his daughter's initial wedding date. Also gone would be Frank's ability to make his way through the life he had built for himself and his family. That would be gone, too, lost forever when David Wilcox's Truck 8 blew Frank's world apart.

The violence of that morning would bring Frank to the brink of death. In fact, several rescuers said he did die, and was brought back to life – a different life – only through the heroic efforts of his passengers, doctors and emergency services workers.

"All I heard is that the guy from the helicopter came by and looked at me and said, 'Don't worry about him, he's dead,'" Frank recalled in an interview about 18 months after the crash. "Dr. Kurtzman came by and saw me bleeding, and he said, 'Let's get on this,' and the paramedics said, 'no, he's dead.' And Dr. K said, 'He ain't dead!' He worked on me, put me in the helicopter, and I didn't know anything for another six weeks of my life."

During that time, Frank's life continued to be in the hands of others, namely Dr. Ronald Gross, the trauma surgeon, and orthopedic specialist Dr. Gerald Becker, both of whom also took care of me. The day after the crash, Dr. Becker met with the Juan family and explained Frank's medical options. They weren't good. The family could decide to do nothing, hoping that Frank would at least survive. However, that choice would almost certainly leave Frank with no chance of walking again. Or they could approve an extremely risky surgery, fraught with the possibility of further worsening Frank's already precarious condition, but that also might restore his ability to walk again someday.

"We were talking about the surgery," said Ramona, Frank's daughter. "And I looked at the doctor and asked, 'What would you do if it was your father?' He said, 'I would do it.' I looked at my brothers and my mom and asked, 'What do you want to do?' She said, 'Let's do it.' So we gave the OK."

But Frank almost didn't make it to surgery. As he was being prepared for the marathon operation, his heart rate plunged. "At one point, they didn't think he'd live long enough to get there," Ramona said. "They brought in a heart specialist, and they were finally able to stabilize him and start surgery."

It would be a long wait for the Juans. The operation began at around 10 a.m. Sunday and lasted until almost midnight. Frank did survive the delicate surgery, which went well enough to yield hope that, with intense rehabilitation, he would regain some mobility. But for the next six weeks, doctors kept him in a coma to help stabilize and heal his broken neck, spinal cord and the other injuries inflicted upon him in the crash.

When he finally regained full consciousness, 40 days after the crash, his first question was, "Why am I here?" Like me, he had no memory of what had happened. When told that he was in a terrible crash at the base of Avon Mountain, his first thought was of his passengers. "Did anyone get hurt?" he asked. "Dad, you were the only one on the bus who got hurt," said his oldest son, Frank, III. "He said, 'Oh, okay.' As long as none of his passengers got hurt, that was his main concern."

A few minutes later, when he realized how much time had passed since he had lost consciousness, he thought of his brother, Richard. "Oh sh--!" Frank remembered saying. "I had to call him because we have a pact; no matter where we are on our birthdays, we will get a hold of each other."

Frank, of course, had a good excuse for missing Richard's call on Aug. 25, 2005, his 66th birthday. But he wasn't going to miss the call for his brother's birthday on Sept. 7. "When I called him, he almost had a heart attack," Frank said, explaining that Richard thought he was still in a coma. "He never expected I would call."

But Frank was indeed alive and alert, although still greatly restricted in movement. Within a few more weeks, he would be moved from Hartford Hospital to Gaylord Hospital in Cheshire, Conn., where he would undergo intense therapy to rebuild strength in his left leg. "I couldn't walk," said Frank, who had lost all feeling from his knee down. "I couldn't do any-thing." Whether he was ever going to be able to walk unassisted was still in question at that point, but it was clear he would never again be able to drive his bus. In addition to losing the ability to support his family – after four decades of working up to 70 hours a week – he also lost what was literally the vehicle for many special times with his family. Over the years, his wife, children and, more recently, his grandchildren, would accompany him on chartered trips to see his beloved Yankees, as well as vacation tours to Cape Cod and Florida.

"We grew up on the bus," recalled Frank's younger son, Michael. "Being on that bus was special time we spent with Dad. His job and his family, that was my dad's life."

Frank was now focused on rehabilitation, but he and Ann also spent a lot of time worrying about medical coverage and whether their Social

Security payments and her part-time job would cover their bills. The family was collecting $313 per week in Workers' Compensation, and was barely making ends meet. Had David Wilcox's Truck 8 been properly insured – not to mention properly maintained, thus avoiding the entire tragedy – the Juans would have had the funds to pay all their bills and then some. But the stark reality was that Wilcox's wretchedly maintained *and* uninsured truck robbed Frank of his ability to walk, to go to the bathroom unassisted, to drive and to earn the money to support his family. It even failed to provide the insurance funds to help with the devastating aftermath.

As it was, the Juans scraped by. And they got a little help from their friends. His passengers chipped in for a total of $1,000 to help Frank. Butch Seitz sold more than 1,500 tickets at $8 each to a fundraising dinner at Scarpelli's Restaurant in Torrington. Virginia Kovaleski and Jaye Giampaolo organized a pasta supper at St. Mary's Church which raised approximately $3,000. Virginia rode Frank's bus periodically, but not the day of the crash. Frank called her "Snowflake" because she rode mostly on snowy days when she didn't want to drive herself. "He's a peach, a wonderful guy," she said.

Maybe that's why he received more than a thousand get-well cards and a steady stream of visitors including, of course, his wife, three children, five grandchildren, two brothers, many friends and bus passengers. All that support, and Frank's naturally upbeat nature, created a sense of optimism as he looked ahead. "Within a year, I'll be perfect," he predicted four months after the crash.

But despite the progress he made through rehabilitation, that year came and went without Frank regaining the ability to walk unassisted. When he finally returned to his Forest Court home in Torrington in January of 2006, six months after he left for work on that fateful summer morning, the boisterous leader of the Juan family was virtually confined to a hospital bed in the center of the family room – a life-long hard-working, energetic, active, macho guy now almost helpless, highly dependent upon those around him for everything. "My father's whole life was getting up, walking out that door and getting in his car and going where he wanted to go," said older son Frank.

By now, Ann's unemployment insurance checks had stopped coming, but because Frank needed her at home she wasn't able to return to work. "I cannot live alone," he said. "I can't. If I try to go to the bathroom by myself, I fall on the floor. If I didn't have my wife, I don't know what I'd do." Meanwhile, the shrinking family budget squeezed them even more. But even with all their struggles, the family was grateful to have Frank home. As the summer of 2006 approached, their focus shifted to Ramona's rescheduled wedding. "I told all my doctors, I said I want you to keep me alive until July 8 because my daughter is getting married," Frank said. "I am too strong to die."

He was. On July 8, 2006, Ramona married Rick Clark in front of Frank, family, friends and the waterfall at Coe Memorial Park in Torrington. "It was awesome," she said. The reception was held a few blocks away at the Knights of Columbus. Three hundred and forty-four days earlier, in the intensive care unit of Hartford Hospital, Ramona had whispered into the ear of her critically injured father, "Dad, please don't go yet. You still have a job to do. Don't go yet, Dad, please don't go." Although he wasn't able to walk her down the aisle as they had dreamed, against incredible odds, Frank was there for his beloved daughter.

"The DJ played 'Daddy's Little Girl,' and I grabbed his oxygen and sat on his lap and my husband just pushed us around the hall," Ramona said. "He said 'thank you' to everyone, and there wasn't a dry eye in the house."

But life soon settled into a routine of dependency and frustration for Frank and his family. He was not happy. That simmering frustration would often boil over into anger and massive stress for Ann, who was now his primary caretaker. "You could walk in the house and my father would be the nicest guy in the world to you," said older son Frank. "But you'd walk out that door and, just like that, he'd turn into a jerk. And he'd take it out on his family, especially my mom. He'd scream and bitch and say he wasn't going to take his pills anymore. She'd finally say, fine, don't take them, and then tell him she was going to have to put him in a convalescent home. Then he'd cry and say he was sorry and didn't mean it."

"There were plenty of nights my mom would call and say she couldn't do it anymore," Ramona said. "She'd say she was going over to her sister's house, that she loved him more than anything, but she just couldn't take it anymore."

One day in October of 2007 Ramona was at work when she received an unexpected phone call. "Daddy's calling me at work. Right then and there I knew something was wrong," she recalled. "He said I need you to come home right away."

Ann Fitzgerald Juan, her mother, Frank's wife and caretaker, had a heart attack and collapsed in the kitchen. "My dad's crying," Ramona said. "He said, 'If anything happens to my wife, I'm telling you, that Wilcox, I'm going to f---ing kill him because it's all his fault! It's too much stress on her to take care of me.'"

"It was so hard," Ramona said. "I mean, I love my dad. I'd do anything for my dad. But if it wasn't for my mother..." Younger brother Michael completed the thought. "She took the brunt of everything," he said.

With Ann in Charlotte Hungerford Hospital, it fell to Ramona to take care of Frank. The first thing she did was, of course, talk with her mom. "So I went to her hospital room and said, 'Alright, Mom, here are Daddy's pills, here's a pencil, here's paper. Tell me what to do. I have no idea,'" Ramona said. "And then his oxygen machine wouldn't work. I'm trying to figure it out. I called Doyle's [medical supply]. I'm a wreck because I'm trying to help my dad, and I'm worried about my mom. My dad is saying, 'Mo, you're doing it wrong.' Dad, this is how they told me. 'Mo, you're doing it wrong.' 'Dad, this is how they told me so just lay there and shut up!' He didn't like that. Finally I said to my brother, 'Frankie, you take over.'"

Within a few days, Ann returned home and continued taking care of her husband. Life didn't get any easier. Frank's mobility was still greatly restricted, but his overall health seemed to level off. Early in the second week in March of 2008, however, Ramona and her husband, Rick, stopped by to visit Frank. "He sounded like he was choking a little," Ramona remembered. "I said, 'Dad, are you alright?' And he's like, 'Yeah, I'm fine.'" She returned a few days later and noticed that her father sounded a little worse. "I said, 'Dad, are you sure you're OK?' And he said, 'What's the worst that could happen? I'll die?'"

The next day, Friday, March 14, younger son Michael called and exchanged a little small talk with his father. "We were talking," Michael said, "and then he said, 'Alright, I love you.' That's when I knew something was wrong. He would say things like 'I love you,' but not right out of the blue. I asked Mom, 'What's wrong with him?' And she said, 'I don't know.'"

Earlier that day, after he ate breakfast, Ann washed him. "Usually after that, he'd fall asleep," Ann said. "But he kept talking and talking. Then he asked me to call his mother. His mother died three years ago." A little later, Frank asked again. "Did you call my mother?" Ann said, "Yeah, I left her a message to call back." He said OK and continued to talk. "At 12 o'clock I asked him if he wanted lunch. He said he wasn't hungry, that he'd have something later. And he kept talking. At around 2 o'clock he said something and I said, 'If you don't shut up, I'm going to come over there and choke you,'" she said, kiddingly.

About an hour later, Ann checked on him. He was gone. For all his talk and volume, for all his joking and teasing, for all his energy and bluster, for all his seemingly endless stream of spirited chatter, Frank died quietly and peacefully in his sleep. "I just sat there on the bed holding his hand," Ann said. "And then I went crazy."

The *Register Citizen* headline read, "Bus driver fondly remembered," the day after the wake. "Mourners filled the Phalen Funeral Home Tuesday evening to say goodbye to Frank Juan, Jr., a well-liked bus driver at Kelley Transit, who survived the 20-vehicle Avon Mountain crash in July 2005. Cars filled the parking lot and lined the streets while people gathered behind the funeral home on Migeon Avenue and shared stories of Juan."[1]

"My father was a great man," said his son Frank. "But he just wanted to die at the end. My father would still be alive if he could work. The reason my father died was because he gave up."

1. *Register Citizen*, March 19, 2008, "Bus Driver Fondly Remembered"

When the family members reflected back, they all agreed that it might have been better if Frank had died the day of the crash. "I said to myself after the crash, well thank God he's alive," Ann said. "But if I knew what he was going to go through for those two and a half years, I started to think that it should have ended at the bottom of the mountain."

Even so, Ann's heart aches for her husband. "Everything that goes wrong today," Ann said, "I keep thinking, if he was here, he'd know what to do."

"She misses him a lot," Ramona said. "They were married 44 years." And, of course, Ramona also deeply misses her beloved dad, the man she always knew would be there for her. "I tell him that I miss him, that I love him," she said about her visits to his grave. "I wish he was still here, but I understand that he didn't want to fight anymore."

The newspapers reported that four people were killed on July 29, 2005. Although the Juan family was spared the brutal shock of a loved one's sudden death, make no mistake that the Avon Mountain crash claimed five lives. The last one belonged to Frank Joseph Juan, Jr., loyal, loving, loud, dedicated and very proud husband, father, grandfather, brother, friend and bus driver.

CHAPTER 14

Plodding toward Justice

If you didn't know any better, you might have thought the slightly rumpled, grey-haired man with glasses and slumping shoulders seated at the defense table in Courtroom A-3 in Hartford Superior Court was just a kindly grandfather. You might have felt a twinge of sympathy. Who was this poor guy? Why was he here?

"All rise!" bellowed the bailiff, announcing the start of the trial. "The State of Connecticut versus David Wilcox. The Honorable Edward Mullarkey presiding."

Wow. The whole state against this poor old man. He looked down at the floor as the judge entered and the assistant state's attorney stood to lead the charge against him, David R. Wilcox, the 72-year-old owner of American Crushing & Recycling (ACR). At this point, that twinge of sympathy might have swelled into a full-blown pang of sadness for him.

And why not? Any compassionate human being with only a barebones understanding of the case before the court might feel that way. If you were one of the nine jurors – three alternates and six primary jurors who would ultimately decide his fate – you could have painted the blank slate that was now Mr. Wilcox with all sorts of imaginings as he stood next to his polished and personable defense attorney Ray Hassett.

But by the time this trial started on May 7, 812 days after Mr. Wilcox's Truck 8 barreled down Avon Mountain and crashed into 19 other vehicles, resulting in five deaths and many more injured, I had had plenty of time to learn about the defendant. So as I sat there on that first day of the trial in the spectators' section of the courtroom, I wasn't buying Mr. Wilcox's body language. Admittedly, I was biased. That's what happens when one of your lungs is punctured and nine bones are broken on your way in to work one morning.

That bias was reinforced by a face-to-face exchange I had with Mr. Wilcox about a year before the start of his insurance-fraud trial. It was my lunch break on April 25, 2007, and I decided to try to talk directly with Mr. Wilcox. So I drove from my ING office in Hartford to ACR in Bloomfield. When I got out of my car, I saw him walking the property with another man. I walked over, introduced myself and said I was in the Avon Mountain crash and was writing a book about it. Mr. Wilcox extended his right hand, and we shook. He was perfectly civil, relaxed, thinner than he appeared in newspaper photos I had seen, mustache neatly trimmed, wearing a Red Sox cap. I asked if we could talk about the crash, that I was interested in his perspective. He politely declined, explaining that his lawyer wouldn't want him to talk about it before the trial. Then he said, "The truth will come out at the trial. I'm sorry about what happened. But the truth will come out at the trial." As I drove away that day, I remember thinking he had convinced himself that the crash wasn't his fault, not even a little bit. That was my gut feeling.

Due to court scheduling issues, the charges against Mr. Wilcox would be pursued in two separate trials. This first trial was about insurance fraud. The more serious charges against him, four counts of second-degree manslaughter and five counts of first-degree assault, would be taken up at a second trial sometime in the future. For now, Mr. Wilcox was facing three specific charges: criminal attempt to commit first-degree larceny, conspiracy to commit first-degree larceny and insurance fraud. The jury knew that these charges were somehow connected to the horrific Avon Mountain crash, which ultimately claimed the lives of five people on that terrible July morning nearly three years ago. But because this case was limited to only Mr. Wilcox's alleged insurance-related actions in the immediate aftermath of the crash, this jury would be allowed to hear from only one person with a direct connection to the actual crash, Jennifer (Spielman) Slade. Her car was among 19 vehicles waiting for the light to change at the base of the mountain. She was not seriously injured.

Even so, her testimony left a deep impression on at least one juror, Katie Robidoux, a student activity account supervisor for Farmington Public Schools. She was one of the three alternate jurors who could fill in for any of the six primary jurors if one of them were unable to fulfill their duties. As an alternate, Mrs. Robidoux would be present for all the court testimony, but would not participate in the juror deliberations that would decide whether or not Mr. Wilcox was guilty of the insurance-related charges against him.

"The light was turning red," Ms. Slade testified. "The truck was in the wrong lane. It was a mass coming down the hill like a rocket. I knew it was out of control. The last I saw of it was when it turned to avoid cars near the Route 10 intersection. It was on two wheels. There was screeching and smashing of rocks. I was waiting for the truck to slam into us, then everything got quiet." She looked up after her head landed in her passenger's lap. She saw people trying to scramble through the windows of the Kelley Transit bus. "Things started exploding," she said.

"I remember her testifying about seeing the truck coming at her," Mrs. Robidoux said. "I felt bad for her. She was visibly nervous and obviously distraught. I could literally 'live it' with her by her testimony. I get goose bumps thinking about her testimony. It was one of the most compelling of the whole trial."

But that would be the last the jury would hear from anyone directly affected by the crash. By the time the primary jurors began deliberating 23 days later, Jennifer Slade's emotional testimony would be buried under an avalanche of insurance policy technicalities and interpretations.

"We were fortunate that Judge Mullarkey allowed Jennifer to testify," recalled prosecutor John Malone after the trial. "He would not have allowed any other victims to testify. It would be different at the manslaughter and assault trial later."

So this jury would not hear about how Mr. Wilcox's Truck 8 devastated the lives of many victims and their loved ones. Nor would they hear directly from Mr. Wilcox. The only way Mr. Malone could question him was if his attorney, Mr. Hassett, put him on the witness stand first. And that was not going to happen. Nor would the jury hear much about Mr. Wilcox's track record of operating his businesses and other issues related to what happened before, during and after the Avon Mountain crash. Due to trial strategy and restrictions, they would not hear about facts such as:

- Donna Wilcox, David Wilcox's wife and office manager, had already been convicted of insurance fraud and conspiracy to commit larceny after pleading no contest on Feb. 29, 2008. She was awaiting sentencing.

- Trucks of David Wilcox-owned companies (Wilcox Trucking Inc. and American Crushing & Recycling, LLC) were cited for 1,136 safety violations in the eight years prior to the July 29, 2005 Avon Mountain crash; 223 times those violations were considered serious enough to have the trucks declared "out of service," which meant they were taken off the road immediately and towed back to a garage.[1]

- According to a police affidavit, "David Wilcox was, on three occasions (March 26, March 30 and June 16, 1999), operating vehicles that were subjected to a roadside Driver Vehicle Examination Report [inspection]. During each of those roadside inspections, David Wilcox was personally cited and declared out of service for operating a commercial motor vehicle without a commercial driver's license. This pattern of his willful and repeated disregard for the Federal Motor Carrier Safety Regulations is evidenced by these inspections, two of which were four days apart."[2]

- On July 17, 2007, Andrew Burnham, whose property was adjacent to Mr. Wilcox's American Crushing & Recycling property at 83 Old Windsor Road in Bloomfield, called Bloomfield Police regarding a property dispute with Mr. Wilcox. During the confrontation,

---

1. Arrest Warrant Affidavit, CFS#: 0500016324, p. 20
2. Arrest Warrant Affidavit, CFS#: 0500016324, p. 17

Mr. Burnham said Mr. Wilcox called him "an outsider and a f----ing n---er."[3]

- On November 22, 2007, Thanksgiving Day, Mr. Wilcox was arrested by Bloomfield Police after Andrew Burnham accused him of trying to run him over on his own property. After investigating, Officer Gerald Thomas arrested Mr. Wilcox for breach of peace, threatening and reckless endangerment.[4]

The Boss

That David Wilcox was the one and only boss at American Crushing and Recycling was pretty clear to former ACR truck driver George Sherman, who testified on that first day of the trial. Mr. Sherman responded to a question from the prosecutor by stating, "Dave had control of everything." His testimony echoed the comment from another former ACR employee, Yvette Melling, who told investigators that "absolutely nothing pertaining to the operation of the company happens without the approval or direction of David Wilcox."[5] "From signing important documents to filling the trucks at 6:30 a.m., Wilcox was the man in charge," Mr. Malone said as he showed the jury documents and witness testimony."[6]

So was it reasonable to believe that Mr. Wilcox did not know that Mrs. Wilcox had canceled the liability insurance on the fleet of ACR dump trucks in early January of 2005? (The suspension of that coverage resulted in a $39,976 refund of premium to ACR's account.[7]) And was it reasonable to believe that on the morning of July 29, 2005 when, in the first 87 minutes after ACR's Truck 8 crashed and burned at the base of Avon Mountain – 87 minutes during which she spoke on the phone to her husband 17 times – that Mrs. Wilcox was *acting on her own* when she asked the insurance company to retroactively reinstate the liability coverage on Truck 8 and the 11 other ACR dump trucks? Was it reasonable to believe that? If you were one of the six primary jurors, you would have to believe that in order to find Mr. Wilcox not guilty.

"Something wasn't right"

The following is just the first 87 minutes of the Wilcox's phone-call record[8] the morning of July 29, 2005:

---

3. Bloomfield Police Department, Case/Incident Report, CFS No. 0700014641
4. Bloomfield Police Department, Case/Incident Report, CFS No. 0700024529
5. Arrest Warrant Affidavit, CFS #: 0500016324, p. 24
6. *Register Citizen*, "Wilcox Insurance Fraud Trial Continues," by Tracy Kennedy, May 9, 2008
7. Arrest Warrant Application, JD-CR-64a Rev. 10-04, pp. 2, 4 b
8. Court transcript, No. CR05-0595432, John McIlhoney, court monitor; pp. 9-10

7:38	ACR's Truck 8 crashes at base of Avon Mountain
7:53	ACR truck driver George Sherman to ACR employee Shaun Wilcox (David's son)
7:53	David Wilcox to Donna Wilcox
7:54	Shaun to George
8:00	David to Donna
8:01	ACR (Donna) to Webster Insurance
8:01	David to Donna
8:02	ACR (Donna) to Noel Janovic (Webster)
8:03	David to Donna
8:04	David to Donna
8:04:40	David to Donna
8:15	David to Donna
8:20	ACR (Donna) to Janovic (leaves message on Janovic's voicemail)
8:20	David to Donna
8:25	David to Donna
8:27	David to Donna
8:27	David to Donna
8:29	ACR (Donna) to Janovic (Webster)
8:31	ACR (Donna) to Janovic (Webster)
8:32	David to Donna
8:35	ACR (Donna) to Janovic (Webster)
8:36	ACR (Donna) to David
8:36	David to Donna
8:38	David to Donna
8:39	David to Donna
8:44	ACR (Donna) to Janovic (Webster)
8:45	ACR (Donna) to Webster (broker's main number)
8:46	David to Donna
8:49	ACR (Donna) to Janovic (Webster)
8:49	ACR (Donna) to Brodeur (Webster)
8:52	ACR (Donna) to Janovic (Webster)
8:54	ACR (Donna) to Janovic (Webster)
8:56	ACR (Donna) to Janovic (Webster)
9:00	ACR (Donna) to Janovic (Webster)
9:05	Donna Wilcox and Noel Janovic speak directly

Noel Janovic, a technical analyst for Webster Insurance Company in Wallingford, Conn., testified for a total of about 11 hours over four days during the trial. She recalled her interaction with Donna Wilcox the morning of the crash.

"I turned on my computer and listened to my voice mail," Ms. Janovic testified. "It was a voice mail from Donna Wilcox left at 8:20 a.m." She was still logging onto her computer when Donna Wilcox called again at 9:05 a.m. Mrs. Wilcox asked Ms. Janovic to reinstate liability insurance on ACR's 12 dump trucks, insurance that was suspended Jan. 4, 2005, Ms. Janovic said. Mrs. Wilcox wanted Webster, acting as a broker, to get the reinstatement from Acadia Insurance Co., retroactive to July 1, 2005, Ms. Janovic said, but Acadia could only reinstate the coverage from 12:01 a.m. of July 29.

"Something wasn't right," Ms. Janovic said. There was something odd about Mrs. Wilcox asking her to fax to her written confirmation, she testified. "Did she ever say, 'By the way, one of the trucks is in an accident?'" asked the prosecutor, John Malone. "Absolutely not," Ms. Janovic replied. But at 10:40 a.m., after Ms. Janovic had processed all the changes Mrs. Wilcox had requested, she received a call from David Wilcox. "He stated that one of his trucks was involved in an accident on Route 44 in Avon," Ms. Janovic said. "He said he didn't know which truck it was. He was shaken up and said Donna Wilcox would call us." Mrs. Wilcox then called with information about the truck.[9]

A Good Witness

The phone records from that morning reveal a long list of opportunities David and Donna had to exchange information just before the insurance fraud was committed. (Remember, prior to her husband's trial, Donna Wilcox had pleaded "no contest" to the insurance fraud charges against her and therefore was convicted of them. But that fact was ruled inadmissable during her husband's trial.) However, the listing of calls doesn't tell you the information that was exchanged during those calls. But surely the jury would connect the well-established dots:

- David was the iron-fisted boss; nothing at ACR happened without his knowledge and approval.

- ACR canceled its liability insurance effective Jan. 4, 2005, and received a $39,976 credit to its account.

- ACR trucks were back on the road within days of that January cancelation, and within days after Truck 8 crashed on July 29, 2005. "If he is allowing his vehicles to be operated without insurance, it is obviously clear he didn't care if he had insurance or not," said Mr. Malone.[10]

---

9. *Register Citizen*, "Insurance Worker Testifies in Trial," Tracy Kennedy, May 10, 2008

10. *Register Citizen*, "More Damaging Testimony Offered," Tracy Kennedy, May 15, 2008

- David and Donna connected on the phone 17 times in 87 minutes directly after the crash.

- In the 88th minute, Donna told the insurance company to retroactively reinstate insurance on the still-smoldering, wrecked Truck 8 that had just killed and/or seriously injured about a dozen people.

One might think those five points would be enough to add up to a guilty verdict. But there was more. After all, although the phone records showed a great deal of activity within a short time, they couldn't reveal what was said during those calls.

Enter Yvette Melling. If the sheer volume of calls between David and Donna Wilcox did not signal something terribly amiss to the jury, then the testimony of Yvette Melling, a former ACR employee, surely would. Or so you would think. Mrs. Melling heard about the crash on the radio during her commute to ACR in Bloomfield that morning.

"Please tell me that wasn't one of our trucks," she said to Donna Wilcox upon arriving in the ACR office at approximately 8 a.m. "She said, 'It must be Number 8 because he [Abdulraheem Naafi] is not answering.'" David Wilcox called his wife and told her to contact the insurance company, Mrs. Melling testified. "(Donna) said she wasn't sure where he was, but that he wanted her to call the insurance company...to reinstate the insurance on the trucks," Mrs. Melling testified. Donna Wilcox told Mrs. Melling that she wanted to call Webster Insurance before it opened to reinstate the insurance. "I was surprised that she would call for insurance after the accident," Mrs. Melling said.[11]

So now the jurors knew a crucial part of the information exchanged during those 17 phone calls between David and Donna Wilcox. And they heard it from a witness who appeared to have a high level of credibility.

"She was one of the best witnesses I've ever had," said Mr. Malone, reflecting back on his 32 years as a state prosecutor. "She was honest, intelligent, and wanted to be fair."

Enter Ray Hassett. Mr. Wilcox's defense attorney graduated from Catholic University of America in 1984 and Quinnipiac College School of Law in 1987. He had served as a special assistant U.S. Attorney before co-founding his own private practice. According to its website, "While the firm of Hassett & George, P.C. has handled matters for Fortune 500 companies, commercial institutions and governmental agencies, each client is treated and dealt with in a personable, professional and accessible manner. At Hassett & George, P.C., each client's matter is of the utmost concern and importance."[12]

---

11. *Register Citizen*, "Wilcox Finances Pored Over in Court," Tracy Kennedy, May 20, 2008
12. http://www.hgesq.com/index.html

Whatever Mr. Wilcox was paying Mr. Hassett, he was getting his money's worth. "If I ever got in trouble, he's the guy I'd hire," said juror Jon Warren after the trial. Whereas Prosecutor Malone was all business/no nonsense, Mr. Hassett was Mr. Personality, taking every opportunity to connect with the jury and even the judge. During his closing argument as he talked about the complexity of insurance documents, Mr. Hassett said, "I submit to you that lawyers grapple with them and struggle with them. Judges occasionally grapple and struggle with them. Not our judge, of course, but other judges do."[13]

Smoke and Mirrors

It was those insurance documents that provided a treasure trove of distraction for a defense attorney who, from my perspective, was looking to steer jurors away from the clear, compelling and damning facts. "Hassett running through documents at a rapid rate," wrote *Hartford Courant* Reporter Loretta Waldman in her live blog. "I'm confused. Can only imagine the juror must be too."[14]

Upon this foundation of ambiguous and bewildering insurance arcana infused with equally baffling legalese, Mr. Hassett built his defense of Mr. Wilcox. For 13 days of trial with 27 witnesses and about 100 exhibits, attorneys Hassett and Malone sparred over the interpretation of certificates of insurance, no-loss letters, the finer points of insurance coverages from comprehensive to bodily injury, and on and on and on.

At one point Judge Mullarkey dismissed the jury to weigh in on the confusing issue of certificates of insurance. While Mr. Hassett was trying to convince the jury that the certificates were proof of insurance, the judge said they were not detailed enough to rely upon.

"The exhibits are mounting by the dozens each day, but defense attorney Hassett said he felt the jury is keeping up with the intricacies of the insurance policies," wrote Tracy Kennedy, a reporter from the *Register Citizen*, based in Torrington, Conn., on May 14.[15]

Mr. Hassett also took issue with the long list of phone calls. "I have a different perception of what happened," he said. During his closing argument, Mr. Hassett classified the calls based on whether they were cell phone calls, calls to or from ACR's regular phone lines or "direct connects," which are similar to walkie-talkie transmissions. Why would that make a difference? Well, anyone near the phone during those direct connects, for example, would hear what was being said. Therefore, David and

13. Court transcript, No. CR05-0595432, John McIlhoney, court monitor; p. 32
14. Hartford Courant.com, Farmington Valley iTowns, Loretta Waldman, live blog, May 29, 2008
15. *Register Citizen*, "Alleged Insurance Fraud Detailed," Tracy Kennedy, May 14, 2008

Donna would presumably not discuss insurance fraud within earshot of a third party such as Yvette Melling. The final slide in the phone call segment of Mr. Hassett's presentation was a big "0" – as in zero opportunities for David and Donna to conspire and discuss insurance fraud.

A masterful sleight of hand, I thought to myself as I sat in the spectators section. But surely the jury would poke holes through Mr. Hassett's interpretation of the phone record. For starters, David and Donna had two phone connections before Yvette Melling's arrival, which was pegged at approximately 8:00 a.m. If that "approximately" allowed for a little leeway, if she, in fact, actually arrived at 8:05 – her exact time of arrival was never nailed down as far as I know – then David and Donna connected six times before anyone else was around to hear them.

Another target for Mr. Hassett during his closing argument was Yvette Melling herself. Put yourself in the shoes of a defense attorney. You really have no choice but to attack a key witness' credibility, right? That's what your client is paying you to do. As hired guns, that's what defense attorneys do. Nothing personal, just business.

So Mr. Hassett dug into the record and found inconsistencies in Mrs. Melling's statements to investigators. In fact, her statements did differ. But why? To understand, put yourself in Yvette Melling's shoes. "I was terrified of him," she said about Mr. Wilcox after the trial. She had personally witnessed the eruption of Mr. Wilcox's volcanic temper many times in the past. She didn't like him, was afraid of him, but considered herself a friend of Donna Wilcox. When it came time to cooperate with investigators and law enforcement, Mrs. Melling did what she believed to be the right and responsible thing to do, despite her family's wishes. They understandably wanted to shield her from the wrath of an angry boss. Based on what they had heard, they thought there was no telling what this man would do. In the absence of a nagging conscience, why would anyone choose to put herself through a grueling process that included sitting and testifying within 20 feet of that angry, glowering boss?

Once she decided to cooperate, Mrs. Melling was interviewed separately over the course of several months by investigators for the insurance company, police, the prosecutor's office and Mr. Hassett's law firm. Mr. Hassett made the most of the differences among Mrs. Melling's statements. The explanations for those differences ranged from the simple – who among us does not recall more details upon further reflection? – to the more complex. For example, Mrs. Melling initially believed that she was allowed to comment only on what she saw or heard herself. She didn't personally observe Donna being told by David to call the insurance company; therefore, she initially said nothing about that.

"Yvette didn't say that because she didn't observe it directly," said prosecutor John Malone after the trial. "She didn't say that Donna told her that David told her to do it. Therefore, some jurors thought she must have made it up. Yvette thought the question asked for her personal observations, not what she was told by Donna. Yvette had no reason, no motivation to lie. She was giving personal, first-hand information, not second-hand information from someone else. As a result, some jurors drew the wrong inference. Yvette was trying to be too careful, trying to be fair."

Nonetheless, to some experienced trial observers, it appeared as though the case against Mr. Wilcox was very strong. Just before the judge was about to issue his final instructions to the jury before deliberations began, Terry Kennedy, court reporter for the *Register Citizen*, turned to me and said, "Bet you five dollars they come back with a guilty verdict in two hours." I took the bet because I thought they would deliberate for at least one full day. It would turn out that we were both wrong.

Getting it Right

Right up until the first day of the trial, Jon Warren thought he was going to be an alternate juror. When the 32-year-old manager for J.C. Penney in Manchester found out he was actually one of the primary jurors, one of six who would have to vote "guilty" or "not guilty" at trial's end, he got a little nervous. "I've got to make sure I get this right," he remembered thinking to himself.

That wasn't going to be easy. "There were times during the trial where I thought, 'Oh my God, what are they talking about?'" Mr. Warren said. "It was very important that you were able to determine what was 'smoke and mirrors' and what was fact."

A substantial portion of the trial was devoted to esoteric aspects of insurance contracts, such as certificates of insurance. "The purpose was to try to make it seem like Wilcox thought he had insurance," Mr. Warren said. "But his wife canceled the liability insurance, they already knew it was suspended. A few weeks into the trial I started to realize, wait a minute, this is all smoke and mirrors. This guy has been running his business all these years. He's been suspending insurance, then putting it back on, then suspending it again. That meant he had a very good awareness and understanding of how insurance policies work. He knew what he was doing."

But at least three of his fellow jurors, including one teacher and one lawyer, were not so sure. One said he didn't believe any of the evidence, period, according to Mr. Warren. Another said she "didn't want to be responsible for sending him to jail," and the third repeatedly would ask, "How do we know?"

They would end up deliberating four days before deadlocking. Three were prepared to vote guilty, three were not. On the final day of their deliberations, Mr. Warren went through a thorough, step-by-step explanation of why he thought Mr. Wilcox was guilty, focusing on all the calls between Donna and David Wilcox the morning of the crash. The three remained unconvinced. So Mr. Warren asked them to explain why they thought he was not guilty. They declined.

Those three jurors wouldn't talk with me, either. Given the opportunity to explain their reasoning, the only response I received was this statement: "There were three jurors who voted not guilty and didn't feel there was anything more that they could offer other than what was in the paper. They felt that there was enough reasonable doubt not to convict."

"Bitterly Disappointed"

"Jurors who deliberated insurance-fraud charges against the owner of a runaway truck that caused a deadly Avon Mountain crash deadlocked because they disagreed on the credibility of a key witness, a juror said Wednesday."[16] That was the lead sentence in the *Hartford Courant* the day after a mistrial was declared.

"They say Yvette's not credible. Where is her interest in the outcome of the case?" asked Mr. Malone during his closing argument. "She doesn't work there anymore...she has no interest one way or the other...it may be that she disliked him...there's a big difference from disliking somebody on the one hand and going into court and lying under oath and subjecting yourself to the penalties of perjury on the other. There's nothing in it for her to do that, to run that risk."[17]

"I was bitterly disappointed," Mr. Malone said after the trial, pledging to not give up on the case.

I had received a phone call that morning with the news that a verdict was about to be announced. I immediately drove toward Hartford, but I was too late. I heard on the radio that a mistrial had been declared. I ended up waiting with reporters outside Courtroom A-3 in Hartford Superior Court to hear what, if anything, Mr. Wilcox was going to say. He finally emerged from the courtroom with his attorney, Mr. Hassett. After listening to a few softball questions and canned replies, I decided to ask a few questions of my own.

Here's how that was reported in the *Hartford Courant*: "But tension spilled outside the courtroom. Mark Robinson, who sustained nine broken [bones] and a punctured lung in the crash, confronted Wilcox about his silence on the tragedy throughout the trial. Wilcox told him, "I've been hurting for years because that's my first and only crash that's ever hurt anyone.""

---

16. *Hartford Courant*, "Prosecutors Vow to Retry Wilcox after Insurance Fraud Mistrial," Katie Melone and Matt Negrin, June 5, 2008
17. Court transcript, No. CR05-0595432, John McIlhoney, court monitor; p. 73

Ray Hassett, his attorney, then silenced him. But Robinson, 51, pressed again, asking Wilcox about his track record of 'a thousand safety violations,' to which Wilcox repeatedly replied, 'That's not true,' as his lawyer interrupted him again."[18]

Well, I guess Mr. Wilcox had me on that one. He didn't have "a thousand safety violations." He had 1,136 of them, if you want to be precise about it.

It would take about ten months, but Yvette Melling and Jon Warren would be vindicated. Time would prove that they were right, and that they had the courage and tenacity to stand up, honor their oaths and fulfill their responsibilities when it would have been immeasurably easier to take a far less demanding path. As far as I know, none of the people who questioned their credibility and reasoning have since offered Yvette and Jon the apologies they so richly deserve.

As difficult as it was for people like Yvette and Jon to participate in the criminal justice system, it can be many times more wrenching for the victims of crime. After suffering through the initial tragedy, victims and their families then must endure a system that often appears to extend every courtesy and benefit of the doubt to the accused at the expense of the victim, including a dysfunctional and increasingly ineffective bond system, unexplained and seemingly endless court delays, and trial rules that often don't allow juries to consider what seems to be very relevant information.

No one has been more brutalized in every sense of the word than Dr. William Petit, Jr. Two parolees invaded his Cheshire home one night in July 2007, beat him with a baseball bat, tied him up and left him for dead. That was just the start of the ordeal that ended with the deaths of his wife, Jennifer, and two daughters, Hayley and Michaela, 17 and 11 years old. The parolees were arrested while fleeing the Petit home after setting it afire.

"Even now, you feel like you are being abused," Dr. Petit said in a newspaper interview in October 2007. "Somebody murders your family in 2007, and they tell you they're going to go to trial in 2010."[19]

Dr. Petit said state prosecutors were prepared to go to trial eight months after the crime. The parolees' taxpayer-financed defense lawyers, however, continue to stall. "It's delay, delay, delay for no apparent reason," he said.[20]

---

18. *Hartford Courant*, "Prosecutors Vow to Retry Wilcox after Insurance Fraud Mistrial," Katie Melone and Matt Negrin, June 5, 2008

19. *Hartford Courant*, "After Tragic Loss, a Soft Voice Speaks Up," Mark Pazniokas, Oct. 26, 2008

20. *Hartford Courant*, "Giving Voice to the Victims," Daniela Altimari, March 5, 2009

CHAPTER 15

Never Forget

Roman Orellana-Melendez didn't have a chance. As the trucker from New Jersey maneuvered his 18-wheel, 65,000-pound, red tractor trailer from Waterville Road/Route 10 onto Route 44 west at the base of Avon Mountain, Sue Kassey – all 5'4" and 125 pounds of her – was ready to pounce.

I was sitting with Officer Kassey in her two-tone, black-and-white Avon Police Department Chevy Blazer just yards away from where David Wilcox's Truck 8 slid to a stop and burst into flames three-and-a-half years earlier. She was there that day, and she remembers. It started with the distinctive ping of 911 calls on the police radio, and then the dispatcher's shorthand description of the reason for all those calls: "truck versus car." Those would be the first hints at the event that would put her life and career on a new path.

Officer Kassey was on patrol in the Huckleberry Hill area of Avon on July 29, 2005. She was one of five on-duty Avon police officers who responded immediately. "It took forever to get to the crash scene," she said. "It felt like an eternity." By the time she was within a few miles of the crash, she saw the column of dense black smoke. "Whoa!" she thought to herself. "The only time I had ever seen anything like that was in the movies. I could hear the flames crackling when I got closer." Sgt. T. J. Jacius, who was already at the scene, said, "Grab your gear, it's bad."

Then Officer Kassey began doing what she was trained to do. "All my training kicked in," she said. Her first task was taking care of Dr. Elena Tomasi, who had just been rescued from her burning car by Todd Myers, a West Hartford police officer.

"She woke me up," said Dr. Tomasi, recalling her memory of Officer Kassey at the scene of the crash. "The first time I opened my eyes, I saw her. She was asking me questions and checking my memory."

Officer Kassey remembers it well. "Elena was almost in shock," she said. "I kept asking her questions to keep her conscious – Where does it hurt? Where do you work?" As she kept the questions coming, Officer Kassey was also assessing Dr. Tomasi's situation. "She had a bad cut on her head. And something had shattered. There was glass on her face. There was a chunk of glass, about the size of a pinkie nail, on her eyeball. I moved it down very carefully, away from her eye."

What Officer Kassey saw that day made a deep impression on her.

"July 29, 2005 was the catalyst for what I do now," she said. And what she was doing now was patrolling the roads of Avon with a keener eye for safety and the new set of credentials she earned after the hands-on help she provided the day of the Avon Mountain crash.

Shortly after the crash, Officer Kassey asked for permission to attend a special training course at the Massachusetts Police Academy in its Department of Motor Vehicle program. After several weeks of intense, on-the-job training, she earned her certification as a motor vehicle inspector. So when the New Jersey trucker with the big red rig drove past us three-and-a-half years after the Avon Mountain crash, Officer Kassey knew exactly what telltale signs of potential trouble she was looking for as she flipped on her flashing lights in pursuit of another big truck.

The tragedy of July 29, 2005 and related developments had set off a predictable round of harrumphing outrage among area politicians.

"I am absolutely livid, and I am utterly appalled," said Gov. M. Jodi Rell about the company owned by David Wilcox, American Crushing and Recycling. "The more I learn about this company the more enraged and horror-struck I become." But David Wilcox's history was no secret. This was a man in charge of companies that had amassed 1,136 safety violations from the state, the same state that also awarded Wilcox with $1.6 million of business.

"On July 29, 2005, one of the most horrific traffic accidents in our state's history occurred at the base of Avon Mountain," wrote Thomas J. Herlihy,[1] the 8th district state senator who had been representing Avon and ten surrounding towns since 1999. "It is my hope that we can use this tragic event as a catalyst to improve safety on Avon Mountain for every motorist who travels it."

With reactions like those, you would have thought that the July 29, 2005 crash was some sort of fluke, an impossible-to-predict, once-in-a-lifetime, unforeseeable aberration. But the seeds of the Avon Mountain calamity had been planted long ago, had taken root, had even poked its dire warnings into broad daylight many times before. The inconvenient fact was that David Wilcox's Truck 8 was the seventh truck in 21 years to plow through the intersection at the base of the mountain after losing its brakes:

Oct. 8, 2001: Dump truck loaded with asphalt loses its brakes while descending Avon Mountain on Route 44 at morning rush hour, slamming into 10 vehicles. Two people were injured.

---

1. Connecticut State Senate Newsletter; Senate Republican website, www.senaterepublican.ct.gov

Sept. 18, 1998: Fertilizer-hauling truck loses its brakes while descending Route 44 into Avon, hitting a car waiting to turn from Nod Road. Two people were injured.

July 26, 1990: Tractor-trailer loses its brakes on Route 44, but avoids hitting a nearby van by roaring over lawns, tearing down power lines and a stoplight and striking a tree. The driver was injured.

April 5, 1990: Tractor-trailer carrying cow manure flips on Route 44 in Avon when its brakes fail while descending the mountain. No injuries reported.

April 22, 1986: Three people hurt, about 150 evacuated when a tanker loses its brakes descending Route 44 into Avon, hitting a car at the Waterville Road (Route 10) intersection and spilling 200 gallons of toxic industrial solvents.

Aug. 9, 1984: Farm truck carrying about 36,000 eggs overturns after careening down Avon Mountain and crashing in Route 10 (Waterville Road) intersection. No injuries, but lengthy cleanup required. [2]

From a broader perspective, you could argue that the State of Connecticut was doing less than ever in terms of protecting the public from dangerous trucks. For example, despite the fact that trucks were travelling more miles on state roads, Connecticut's roadside truck inspections had dropped dramatically. "Overall, roadside truck inspections carried out by the state dropped 30 percent between 2002 and 2004, according to the Federal Motor Carrier Safety Administration, with the most-thorough roadside inspections dropping by an even greater amount. And comprehensive on-site 'compliance reviews,' in which investigators examine a trucking company's records and its entire fleet, have plunged – from 118 in 2002 to just 24 in the first 11 months of 2004."[3]

To be sure, after decades of legislative and local foot-dragging, some short-term safety improvements were made on Avon Mountain after the July 29, 2005 crash, including better traffic signs, the addition of police ticketing areas, and pavement surface improvements at some of the sharper curves.

State-wide improvements were also implemented. For example, the Department of Motor Vehicles (DMV) began offering a "Trucks 101" program, which teaches police basic truck safety procedures. More municipal

2. *Hartford Courant*, p. A8, July 30, 2005, "Dangers of Busy Road, Steep Grade, Heavy Trucks"
3. *Hartford Courant*, "Truck Inspections Decline Sharply," Matthew Kauffman, Aug. 2, 2005

police officers were now qualified to do truck inspections, supplementing the DMV's 118 certified inspectors and 69 state police inspectors.[4]

More high-profile efforts to enforce road safety would also periodically take place. Just prior to the one-year anniversary of the Avon Mountain crash, for example, the state implemented "Roadcheck 2006," a three-day safety crackdown targeting commercial trucks and buses that were violating various federal and state regulations. In addition, four new truck safety laws went into effect in July 2006, which gave state officials increased authority over drivers and their companies that failed to meet safety standards.[5] And Avon Police instituted "Operation Rush Hour" in February 2006 to focus on unsafe driving. About 4,000 drivers were stopped on the mountain, and about a third of them were fined.

These were all welcome, if not overdue, efforts to help make motorists safer. However, they were not nearly enough. Work had still not begun on a long-delayed road-improvement plan for the 3.1 miles of Route 44 that traverses Avon Mountain, where 14 people had died in crashes since 1995.[6] After the July 29, 2005 crash, Avon asked state and federal agencies to accelerate their planned timetable for implementing a $7 million proposal by the Capital Region Council of Governments, which called for widening Route 44 and installing shoulders and medians.[7] Other suggestions, such as an automatic camera system to enforce speed limits and a runaway truck ramp, appeared to be going nowhere.

But it would take yet another major wake-up call to finally ignite a greater sense of urgency, as if the seven previous truck crashes in 21 years weren't enough. On Sept. 7, 2007, my wife Chris and I were on Cape Cod when just before noon both of our cell phones began ringing. Had we heard? Yet another truck had barreled down the mountain and through the intersection at its base. Miraculously, no one was killed. The driver managed to thread the proverbial needle by veering slightly to his left as he approached the crowded intersection where my mother-in-law, Helen Silansky, was waiting at the traffic light.

"I was on Waterville Road [Route 10] coming from Farmington, and about to turn left onto Route 44 going west toward Avon," she said. "There were three cars ahead of me. All of a sudden, I heard a loud honking and saw a blur fly through the intersection just in front of us." Then there was the sound of the crash.

---

4. *Hartford Courant*, "For Officers, the Truck Stops Here," Christine Dempsey, Aug. 19, 2007

5. US Fed News Service, "Gov. Rell Announces New Truck Safety Laws in Effect;" July 1, 2006

6. *New York Times*, "On a Mountain Road in Connecticut, Hazards and Headaches," Ken Belson, Sept. 30, 2007

7. *Hartford Courant*, "Expedited Route 44 Upgrade Sought," Daniel P. Jones, Aug. 5, 2005

Driver Robert Rauch, 44, from Jersey City, N.J., lost his brakes coming down the mountain, veered into the opposite lane to avoid cars in front of him, miraculously maneuvered his tractor and flatbed trailer loaded with roof shingles through the intersection without smashing into anyone, then flew over a small grassy embankment, somehow managing to hit a narrow gap between trees and telephone poles before finally crashing into the showroom of Nassau's Furniture store.

Once again, local conversation was dominated by another Avon Mountain crash, the eighth time in 23 years that a truck had lost its brakes descending Avon Mountain and barreled through a crowded intersection at the base. WTIC radio host Ray Dunaway interviewed several area politicians within hours of the crash.[8]

Dunaway: So what happened after the events of two years ago (the July 29, 2005 Avon Mountain crash)?

Kevin Witkos, 17th District State Representative, covering Avon and Canton: "They did a few things. They moved up from 2010 to 2008 the [planned] improvements to the highway itself. They created some turn-out lanes for the police to pull people over safely to enforce speeding and other moving violations. They put signage up, changed the surface of the roadways in case someone is sleepy it might wake them up, it rattles a bit. But that's all that's been done. And obviously we saw this morning that that doesn't correct the problem.

Dunaway also interviewed State Senator Tom Herlihy.

Dunaway: Here we are again...after the incident two years and two months ago, you were pretty strong on this and said, 'Look, we've got to do something about it.' And so we started ticketing, and doing more speed enforcement. And that's a good thing. We've got these nifty signs on top of the mountain; there was talk of runaway truck lanes. But here we are two years later and another one...Tom, what do you say?

Herlihy: I sent a letter to the DOT [Department of Transportation] today, copied the governor, the leaders of the General Assembly, chair and ranking members of the Transportation Committee. We need to shut the mountain to large commercial vehicles. We need a moratorium of indefinite length. We need to reconvene that Avon Mountain task force. And we need to get the DOT, which is planning improvements and renovations to the mountain in 2008, we need them to start immediately. Those are the first three things that I'm calling upon. And I'm just hoping that we'll do everything in our power to make that mountain safe for the people who live around there.

Dunaway: What about those truck ramps? Did you look into that?

Herlihy: We can't get a big box store built. We're going to get a runaway truck ramp put on somebody's front lawn...or near someone's property?

8. WTIC Radio, Ray Dunaway interview, Sept. 7, 2007

The DOT says it has taken a look and tried to check to see if it's feasible and have determined that it's not...I don't think that's the answer. I just don't see us ending up with that runaway truck ramp ever getting built.

Thirteen days later the state announced it would go forward with plans to build a runaway truck ramp on Avon Mountain. It was built and operating five-and-a-half months later. A temporary ban on large trucks going over the mountain was also implemented.

On the day of the Nassau's crash, the lawyer representing Chip Stotler's estate, Michael Stratton, said he had heard right away from several survivors of the 2005 crash. "I've gotten a lot of e-mails, and there's a real sense of anger and a lack of comprehension as to why the state hasn't moved faster to remedy the problems on the roadway," Stratton said.

The quick response after the Sept. 7, 2007 crash into Nassau's was a noticeable difference from past practice. "The action stands in sharp contrast to the more measured response after a July 2005 accident that left four people dead,"[9] wrote Katie Melone in the *Hartford Courant*.[10] "In the two years since that accident, the DOT erected signs on the mountain and drafted plans for an overhaul of Route 44 set to start in the spring, but it appears it has not collected any information about the type of trucks that traverse Avon Mountain, and most of the big-picture solutions proposed went nowhere. State officials say the ramp idea was scuttled because of Avon's concerns about the project."

"We had proposed this after the 2005 accident," said Jude Everhart, DOT spokesman. "The town was not receptive to that idea, so it didn't go forward."

But the Sept. 7, 2007 crash into Nassau's showroom proved to be the tipping point. Most people in a position to make the ramp happen got on board and made it happen. The new ramp opened on Feb. 21, 2008. It is not nearly the magic bullet for the traffic problems on Avon Mountain, but I think it's progress and part of the overall eventual solution, which includes all motorists driving more carefully.

Even if one had existed, no one will ever know if Abdulraheem Naafi would have steered his truck onto a runaway ramp the morning of July 29, 2005. People have criticized the new ramp's short, narrow look, arguing that it might not be effective. But given the choice of veering onto a ramp or flying straight toward the crowded intersection, the odds are pretty good that Raheem would have used that heartbeat in decision time to choose the ramp. The families of Chip Stotler, Maureen Edlund, Barbara

---

9. Kelley Transit bus driver Frank Juan, who was critically injured in the July 29, 2005 crash, died March 14, 2008; therefore, some say that five lives were ultimately claimed by the July 29, 2005 crash

10. *Hartford Courant*, "DOT Gears Up for Truck Escape Ramp," Katie Melone, Sept. 20, 2007

Bongiovanni, Abdulraheem Naafi and Frank Juan sure wish he had had that option, that those in a position to make it happen had acted with more urgency and hadn't waited until the eighth truck in 23 years barreled down the mountain and through the intersection at its base, putting yet another group of random innocents at grave risk.

✧ ✧ ✧ ✧

Sure enough, there was a bit of a wobble in the driver-side rear wheels of the New Jersey-plated tractor-trailer that had just passed Officer Kassey and me.

"He knows I'm coming after him," Officer Kassey said as she maneuvered her Avon PD Chevy Blazer with lights flashing to a clear line of sight into the truck driver's side-view mirror. Then she pulled in front of the truck, a Volvo tractor with a long red trailer, motioning the driver to follow her to a parking lot on Hopmeadow Street. "In my experience, I've found that some makes are notorious for drag-link, steering-arm issues; once that snaps, you're in big trouble."

All her senses, and occasionally a little intuition, come into play when Officer Kassey scans trucks driving past her. "Sometimes there's something visible," she said. "Sometimes you can smell potential trouble, like the burning brakes on an auto transporter recently that turned out to be missing brake parts. And sometimes, it's just a gut feeling."

Avon Police had always carefully patrolled the heavily traveled Route 44 corridor favored by many motorists and truckers as they pass through the town on their way to somewhere else. But after the July 2005 crash, there was "a new normal for us," Officer Kassey explained, citing a greater emphasis on proactive safety. Her increased vigilance was one example of Avon's greater focus on monitoring truck traffic.

In 2008, Officer Kassey inspected 312 trucks and put 164 of them "out of service" due to some serious violation. "Rules are rules," she said. "One guy recently didn't have his tag axle down [an additional two wheels to help steady trucks carrying large loads]. He had a full load. I followed him for half a mile; he didn't put it down. The guy ended up with a $9,800 fine."

Truck inspections are tedious, hands-on work; each one takes approximately an hour. At first, Officer Kassey felt a little overwhelmed. "I remember thinking, 'holy smoke,' she said. "But I really do like my job. I don't care what the weather is, sun or rain. The goal is to get bad trucks off the road."

On this day in February 2009, it's sunny and cold, about 30°F. With the New Jersey truck now safely off the road, Officer Kassey gets ready to conduct yet another inspection. She averages approximately 30 a month. "I'm nosy," she said. "I want to see what's going on, so I poke around and try to get the driver to talk to me. They tell you things. I'm always nice to them. I'm in a position of power, so there's no need to be nasty. But I don't let these guys slide. I'm not out here to be taken advantage of. I'm out here to make sure everyone gets home safely, including the truck driver."

First things first. Officer Kassey puts wedges behind the rear wheels of the trailer, then starts talking to the driver, Roman Orellana-Melendez. After a few minutes, she returns to the Avon PD Chevy Blazer with the driver's license and log book. She can't find the license on the computer system. "Roman, what's going on with you?" she said before asking the dispatcher to help check the license number.

Meanwhile, the driver sits patiently in his cab playing a video poker game. Mr. Orellana-Melendez is 35 years old, a truck driver for seven years, and seems like a very nice guy. He picked up the trailer this morning at a pier in New Jersey. "I'm doing my best to drive safely," he said. "I'm happy. I like driving. I try to be safe out there. You've got to take it easy."

It turns out that there's no problem with his license or his record as a driver. Officer Kassey once again gets out of the Blazer and begins the physical inspection of the truck itself, literally getting all over it, and under it, too. She checks the lights, horn and fire extinguisher. She asks the driver to "rock wheels" as she checks the steering, then the air pressure on the brake system. She checks all the tires, including lug nuts and rims. Her practiced eye carefully scans the entire truck.

Next, she takes her "mechanic's creeper," a sled-like plastic board with little wheels that allows her to lie on her back, slide under the truck and inspect the axles, air chambers and brake linings. Ultimately, she determines that "this is a good truck, nothing stands out."

When she emerges from under the truck, she turns over the mechanic's creeper to show me something she has written in black marker on its underside:

7/29/05

Never Forget

CHAPTER 16

"Thank You"

It was about a week after the Avon Mountain crash. West Hartford Police Officer Todd Myers was already back into his normal routine. While tending to some paperwork in a back office at the police station, he was summoned to the front desk; someone was there to see him.

At first he didn't recognize his visitor. The last time Todd had seen her she was "a bloody, mangled mess," he said.

Someone from the Avon Police Department had spoken to Dr. Elena Tomasi's sister. "She told her what happened, who saved me," Dr. Tomasi said. "She said the officer was Todd Myers."

What do you say to the person who saved your life? If you're Elena Tomasi, you say "thank you." And if you're Todd Myers, that's more than enough.

"She's really, really a great lady," he said. "I was overwhelmed by her visit and gesture. That had never happened before. I spent 20 minutes with her explaining what happened and her injuries. She also sent me a really nice thank-you letter. I was stunned."

It wouldn't be the last surprise for Todd Myers. About two years later, he got a call from the U.S. Justice Department. That's when he found out that West Hartford Police Chief James Strillacci had nominated him for the Public Safety Officer Medal of Valor for his off-duty action at the scene of the Avon Mountain crash. On Dec. 12, 2007, he was one of only five people nationwide to receive the award, which included an Oval Office visit with President George W. Bush.

"I was shocked by the whole thing," Todd said. "It was a thrill."

Todd's wife, Megan, a graduate of Smith College and a school psychologist for Farmington Public Schools, remembered her husband's initial reaction after finding out about the award. "We were home, sitting on the couch, and he kept saying he didn't understand why he was getting it," Megan said. "I told him, 'There's a person walking around on this planet right now because of what you did.' He said, 'Yeah, OK.'"

Megan believes that even with the dramatic rescue of Dr. Tomasi, her husband is still haunted by what happened that day. "I don't think Todd is satisfied with the outcome," she said, "because they couldn't get to everyone." He didn't disagree. "We just couldn't do it," he said.

Truck 8 had split the crash scene in two. One cluster of vehicles hit by the 50,000 pounds of fill was smashed in and around the Kelley Transit bus. About 25 yards away was the second cluster of vehicles, those hit directly by the truck and dragged along its final path.

Within those two clusters, up to eight life-or-death struggles unfolded simultaneously.

Megan said she's very proud of her husband. At the same time, "I wish he wouldn't beat himself up over things he had no control over, or that didn't go the right way," she said. "There are a few ways to think about it. First, his actions saved someone's life. But he's also thinking about what he didn't do, what he couldn't do, what there wasn't time for. I wish he wouldn't do that so much. Physically, it was just impossible to simultaneously rescue everyone at the same time."

Megan Myers isn't the only one who fully appreciates the heroic actions of her husband. "I was saved only because of Todd's fast response, courage and professional training," said Dr. Tomasi. "He evaluated the situation quickly, and gave everyone who was there an assignment; he told them what to do."

The aftermath of the crash was difficult for Dr. Tomasi's husband and son. "They get emotional," she said. "I think the spouses react more than we did. My husband didn't recognize me at first in the hospital. He was very emotional."

As for herself, Dr. Tomasi has a new perspective. "I look at life differently," she said. "I was saved. I probably have an important mission in life, maybe something like the 'Doctors Without Borders' program, or maybe to be here for my son. Everything has a reason. I was saved for a reason. This experience has made me ask, 'What is my destination?'"

CHAPTER 17

"A Wonderful, Wonderful Mother"

Tara Edlund found a $20 bill on the factory floor of Jacobs Vehicle Systems one day. She had recently graduated from Hobart College and was living with her mother, Maureen, for a few months, and working a summer job at Jacobs. She brought it to her mother, who was the company receptionist.

"I thought about just sticking it in my pocket, but I decided to turn it in," Tara said. "When I did, my mom was so happy. She said, 'Tara, now I know that I have completed my goal. I wanted you to be a college graduate and a good, honest person. And you just proved that you are.'"

That $20 will pay a lifetime dividend for Tara. "I think about that phrase now because it lets me know that I fulfilled her expectations of me," Tara said.

No parent was more devoted than Maureen Edlund. On the morning of July 29, 2005, she was running a few minutes late on the way to her full-time job at Jacobs in Bloomfield after another late night at her part-time job at Wal-Mart in Avon. David Wilcox's Truck 8 put an end to Maureen's mission to finish paying for her daughter's education, to her dedication to her ailing mother, to her passion for painting, to her chance to be at her beloved daughter's July 2009 wedding to Andrew Scott.

"My mom was usually tired," Tara said. "She would work a full week at Jacobs, work three nights a week at Wal-Mart, spend the whole day Saturday taking care of her elderly mother, and then work another eight hours on Sunday at Wal-Mart. Painting was her true escape during this time."

Like many recent college graduates, Tara did not immediately find a job to match her newly minted degree and career aspirations. Her mom helped her get that temporary summer position at Jacobs, which needed extra help during the vacation season as many of its employees took time off.

"I worked in the manufacturing area doing line work," Tara said. "Not very glamorous, but it paid well. Because we were working in the same place with the same hours, my mom and I ended up spending a lot of time together that summer. Almost every day she would come and sit with me outside during my lunch break. I worked many weekends, too, but my mom would pick me up afterward, and we would just 'hang out' together. Although I was a little grumpy that summer from all the hard work, I now look back on it as one of the best times I had with my mom."

Those days working together with her mom also included that morning commute along the scenic route beside the Farmington River on Nod Road, the same route Maureen was taking July 29, 2005.

"She never went home that way, only to work," Tara said. "That's what my mother was doing that Friday morning in July – the same thing she had been doing for 14 years [since the death of her husband and Tara's father], trying to find a little peace and beauty in her otherwise overcommitted life. She was planning on going to work, being a friendly face, a good neighbor, a wonderful, wonderful mother, a dutiful and all-around great person, just as she had been her entire life."

CHAPTER 18

"It Wasn't a Forever Good-bye"

The night before she died, Barbara Bongiovanni visited her son Vincent in his Torrington apartment. Just before she left, after a hug and a kiss, she turned to Vincent and said, "Good-bye for now, I'll see you soon."

With every fiber of his being, Vincent believes that he will indeed see his beloved mother again. "It wasn't a forever good-bye," he said of that last visit. "There in my little apartment in the kitchen, we sat for what would be the last time in this world and read together from the Bible, and prayed to God for strength and wisdom," Vincent said. "I love my mother and praise God that I will see her again."

"She was an angel," said Barbara's 90-year-old Aunt Celia. "She was always stopping by to see me."

David Wilcox's Truck 8 ended those visits to her son, to her Aunt Celia, to her ailing mother Carmella, to her older brother Floyd, to her little family of coworkers at Saint Francis Hospital. It also put an end to her plans to marry her fiancé, Ted Connole.

"She'd go out of her way for people," Ted said. "She had a good sense of humor. She was great with kids, the elderly. She cared a lot about her co-workers. She was caring, she was a giver. She had the misfortune of a lot of bad events in her life. It just seemed that she had gotten through it all."[1]

He met her at a party in Winsted about five years before the crash, and was taken by her charm and zest for life. Among her many interests were gardening and health, everything from exercise to practicing reiki, a treatment used to help reduce stress and promote relaxation.

That zest for life was one of the many reasons her Saint Francis colleagues deeply mourned her death. "She was genuine," said Della Copeland. "She didn't have a bad bone in her body. If you knew her, you loved her. It's hard to find people like that, who you can say: she's just a good person."

Her greatest passion, perhaps, was her son Vincent and the strong faith they shared in God. "She was very protective of Vinnie," said colleague Sylvia Milner. "He was such a light in her life."

It's that faith that has sustained Vincent. "I can rest today knowing that my mother is with the Lord," he said.

He believes his mother's dream lives on through him and his

---

1. *Hartford Courant*, August 2, 2005, "Torrington Woman is Third Crash Victim Identified"

involvement with "The Bridge," a Christian arts center. "She always dreamed of helping people," he said. "The Bridge is truly helping people discover their purpose in life and see their dreams realized."

The center offers dance training, martial arts, a recording studio, a healthy juice bar and live performances every Friday night. (For more information, see www.thebridgect.com.) Vincent also has a ministry called The New Tribe of Judah, which is working to help eliminate poverty and show people how to live more prosperously. (For more information, see www.TNTOJ.com.)

"I plan to continue to live a life that honors my Lord and my mother," Vincent said. "She may be gone, but her love will live on."

CHAPTER 19

Ripple

"Chip was a lot of things to a lot of people.
But he was everything to the girls and me."

— *Ellen Stotler*

If the measure of a man is the sum of genuine love, goodwill and leadership he provided through countless acts of kindness, affection, guidance, fellowship and good cheer, then Chip Stotler was the richest man in town.

As those who knew Chip were suddenly confronted with the dreadful, mind-numbing thought of life without him, their attempts to comprehend the incomprehensible led to a massive outpouring of grief and mutual support. Family, friends, colleagues, students, neighbors, casual and long-ago acquaintances – they all felt the deep need to participate in the grieving process. How many people who have left this earthly existence have had their dry cleaner show up at their wake?

"The support we've gotten from people has been overwhelming," said Chip's younger brother, Johnny, shortly after the crash. "I just want to thank everyone. We knew Chip reached out to a lot of people, but to see so many of them at once really brought it home."

Hundreds of people attended Chip's wake, and many dozens wrote their remembrances and condolences in an electronic guest book. One of Chip's favorite songs was a tune by the Grateful Dead, "Ripple" – perhaps the perfect metaphor for the positive effect Chip had on so many.

"Few people can leave the world so young and have had such an inspiring impact on the lives of so many," wrote Toni Johnson from Uncasville, Conn.

"Chip was always up for staging a well-thought-out prank, and the best part was that they were both harmless and funny!" wrote Charles Blow, New Hartford, Conn. "I stand today in awe at the sheer number of lives that Chip had a positive effect on. He was truly an amazing man!"

"You could tell by the way he looked and played with the girls that he was a truly terrific Dad who loved his family very, very much," wrote the Wilkinson family, New Hartford, Conn. "He touched so many people's lives with his kind heart and love of life. I will always remember him bouncing out of Giant Steps [daycare center], engineer's hat on, huge smile, and with his girls in tow. When you close your eyes and think of Chip, you can't help but smile."

"I had the honor of meeting Chip when I was at the Gengras Center," wrote one of his former students, Josh Mears, Wolcott, Conn. "I was in the Class of 2002. I really enjoyed his endless friendship. He was the one who got me hooked on the 'BillyBob teeth.' We had great times with those really funny teeth. I am going to miss him a lot. He will always have a special place in my heart. Rest in peace, Chip, buddy of mine, friend of mine."

Somehow Ellen – Chip's high school sweetheart, his wife, his best friend of more than 20 years, and now his widow – was able to find the strength to address the people who filled Immaculate Conception Church in Norfolk, Conn. for his funeral. "Chip was a lot of things to a lot of people, but he was everything to the girls and me," she told everyone. "He guided us. He was our rock and our security and our very own comedian."

According to Mike Gessford, one of Chip's Gengras Center colleagues, "Ellen and Chip were matched souls. He was always expressing how lucky he was to have her."

In a thank-you note she wrote later to family, friends and acquaintances, Ellen said, "While there is nothing anyone can say or do to ease our pain, the amazing amount of love, support and prayers we have received – some from people who have never met us – is inspiring. And just as words cannot express the magnitude of our loss or the sorrow everyone feels for us, words cannot express the appreciation we have for all who have shown us such kindness and generosity."

✧ ✧ ✧

Bobbie Stotler had an unexpected visitor during a visit to her son's grave on the one-year anniversary of his death. Justin McGlamery, a Gengras Center colleague, pulled up with his wife and young daughter. Chip had been a mentor to Justin, showing by example how to connect and collaborate with students, fellow teachers and administrators.

"Chip's running line was 'thanks for coming in today, you're doing a good job,'" Justin said. "He showed me the importance of not taking things too seriously." Justin didn't want to intrude on Bobbie's visit, but she was very happy to see him. "I was very grateful for all the hugs I got from Justin and his family," Bobbie said.

"Chip touched people in a way they weren't even aware of until he was gone," Justin said. "I think about him all the time. His influence continues to have a profound effect on me and many others."

"His Whole Life Was a TORB"

Going back to school in the fall means the end of summer and the start of a new school year. The Gengras Center faculty and students were going to face the enormous challenge of carrying on without their "friendly giant." One colleague felt the immediate need to revisit the campus.

"The day after the crash, I was drawn back there," Mike Gessford said about the playground area and a bench he and Chip built together, the one they finished the day before the crash. Or at least Mike thought it was finished. "I came back and had to leave my little tribute to Chip. He was so proud of the bench because of its curved seat. He was a great woodworker. The log had been sitting around for a couple of years, and Chip always knew he wanted to make it into a bench. I came to sit on the bench, and I sat on it and fell right over backwards because one little piece was missing. I said, 'Chip, I know you did that!' I was laying there with my feet up in the air laughing. One last prank from Chip. That day, I wrote in the back of the bench my little message. It says, 'Chip, that's a TORB. Rest in peace brother, Mike.' A TORB is a Chip-ism, a 'Thing Of Rare Beauty.' His whole life was a TORB."

Eventually, the playground Chip helped build for students was rededicated as the "Chip Stotler Adventure Education Area." On that dedication day, all students, faculty and members of the Stotler family were given engineer's caps. One single cap was suspended on a climbing rope above the outdoor education area. A few staff members played some of Chip's favorite songs, including "Ripple" and everyone sang along.

They also played a game that day. It started with a little blue racquetball that a few students passed over a wall. Then another group of students hiding on the other side of the wall suddenly passed a gigantic, six-foot-high blue ball back over the wall, symbolic of Chip's message that when you share an idea, it becomes bigger and bigger. They rolled the ball through the Gengras Center and people attached sticky notes with new ideas and remembrances of Chip.

"Chip Stotler had little use for convention; he was too busy living life," wrote "The Gengras Center Community" in an essay entitled *Remembering our friend*. "He had the wisdom that comes with mastering the art of living, and he freely shared it with everyone he met. In truth, all of us at The Gengras Center were his students. We were drawn to his charisma the way eager students attend to gifted teachers. We studied him, hoping to find the secret to one of life's largest questions: How can I be truly happy? It was obvious Chip had the answer."

"Chip danced through life," the essay continued. "He was deaf to the static sounds of pettiness. He had room for everyone: the healthy, the infirm, even those who just happened to be close at hand were swept up... Chip showed us life properly lived; he told us with acts more powerful than words, 'Now you try it.'"

Those acts included everything from his little pranks – announcing in a very serious tone over The Gengras Center public address system that "there are no announcements at this time" – to insisting that a new colleague take his reserved parking space for the duration of her pregnancy.

People walking near the Connor Chapel of Our Lady on the campus of Saint Joseph College in West Hartford on Sept. 21, 2005 might have thought a party was taking place inside. And in one sense, they would have been right. Technically, it was a memorial service for Chip, highlighted by his colleagues sharing their memories – many of which made the attendees, including members of the Stotler family, literally laugh out loud.

There was Bernie Lindauer, the serious, no-nonsense leader of The Gengras Center, standing at the church pulpit in a "Surfer Dude" t-shirt. "I want to tell you a story about how I got it," he dead-panned, as he began telling a "tall tale" in Chip-like fashion. "For my 50th birthday back in June 2000, Chip surprised me with a trip I'll never forget. We left Gengras Center Friday after dismissal. We hopped a plane to Hawaii. We spent 18 incredible hours surfing in Maui. Chip was amazed to find that I shared the same passion...and that I was a triathlete in college." Everyone laughed, knowing by now that this truly was a fanciful bit of fiction. "We partied all night," Bernie continued. "We got back to the Gengras Center a little late on Monday, but we were able to keep the secret of our wild weekend for five years. The lesson: there's more to people than what meets the eye."

Jeff Dutko stood up to recite a variation of the Bullmoose Society pledge. "I'd like everyone to raise their dominant hand," he said, initiating perhaps the first-ever Bullmoose pledge in the Connor Chapel, or any other chapel for that matter. "Do you solemnly swear to uphold the bylaws of the Bullmoose Society? Do you solemnly swear in good times and bad, in sickness and in health, from this point forward, in honor of Chip, that you will drink any drink, young or old, hot or cold, with your non-dominant hand?" Most responded with a hearty "I do!" which means that forever more, if they are caught drinking with their dominant hand, they can be "bullmoosed" by a fellow member. When that happens, the offender must chug whatever they happen to be drinking – warm beer, hot coffee, whatever – right at that moment.

Laurel Kendzior told the story of a recent trip Gengras Center seniors had made to Camp Jewel. "One thing Chip said was really taken to heart by our big kids. He said, 'Everyone deserves a cool friend.' Chip was a cool friend, and we're going to miss him very much."

Father David Cinquegrani, who was leading the memorial service, said the symbol of life is a candle. Three people got up to light candles near the altar to start that part of the ceremony, but the candles simply would not light. The more they tried and failed to light them, the more the congregation laughed. Bobbie Stotler told everyone that Chip was somehow behind this.

Sister Agnes Kiely was asked to do the ceremony's concluding tribute.

"I thought the people who knew him best could tell me what made them grateful that he was their friend," she said. "The following are precious thoughts that members of The Gengras Center shared with me. I am grateful for their sharing. After each thought, I'd like everyone to respond with the phrase 'Thank you, God.'"

"Chip was an administrator and, as such, he had a very relaxed side of him that established rapport and trust. He was very supportive and helpful, understanding others' points of view. For this we say...

"Thank you, God.

"Chip was solid, steady and reliable, firmly grounded, calm, cool and collected. For this we say...

"Thank you, God.

"Chip had an inner goodness. He dealt with things with an inner peace. For this we say...

"Thank you, God.

"Chip learned the good lessons and he wanted others to learn from his mistakes. He used humor that was often filled with wisdom. For this we say...

"Thank you, God.

"Chip had the ability to slow things down, and put them into perspective, and help us to see the bigger picture. He was a very good listener. He would wait patiently until we were able to say whatever needed to be said. For this we say...

"Thank you, God.

"Chip taught us by example to show no judgment of other persons. He taught us to find and nurture the best qualities of people, and to focus on those qualities. For this we say...

"Thank you, God.

"Chip found his own common link with each person, whether he was surfing, skiing, woodworking or talking about Vermont or adventure education. For this we say...

"Thank you, God.

"Chip was a man who knew the importance of fun, laughter, hard work and friendship. Whether you had a small problem, or one that was more complicated, Chip was always willing to do whatever he could to help. For someone who had so many responsibilities, he was amazing at making you feel that your immediate problem was important. He always made you feel that he wanted to help because he cared and was compassionate, and not because it was his job. For this we say...

"Thank you, God.

"Chip was also known for giving head butts and giant bear hugs. For this we say...

"Thank you, God.

"Chip taught us what it meant to love family. He adored his own family. He loved the Gengras family, as well as the extended family of Saint Joseph College. He lived his life well, and left a lifetime of friendships. For this we say...

"Thank you, God."

CHAPTER 20

"It Wasn't Your Time, Bro'"

The North Central Municipal Accident Reconstruction Squad meets once a month to review recent cases and stay abreast of new developments. I was invited to attend its Jan. 14, 2009 meeting at the Simsbury Police Station. Among the things I saw that day were more pictures of the Avon Mountain crash. One in particular – a photo of the interior of my 2001 Mercury Cougar – brought me back to a day in September 2005, a few months after the crash. I was still wearing a brace, which stabilized my mid section to help heal six broken ribs and two broken vertebrae.

Ostensibly, I wanted to retrieve a few things from my demolished car, which had been taken to a junkyard near the Berlin Turnpike. I think what I really wanted that day was to just look at my car. A tall, burly young guy wearing a New York Yankees baseball cap led me to it. I fixated on the large chuck of concrete that blasted through the windshield and landed on the passenger seat. I'm guessing I had a horrified expression. After a few moments, the young guy looked at me and said, "It wasn't your time, bro."

I appreciated the gesture. And I'd like to think that maybe there's something to the notion that "it wasn't my time." But every time I hear that, the doubts come rushing in. Why was it time for Chip Stotler, Maureen Edlund, Barbara Bongiovanni, Abdulraheem Naafi and Frank Juan? Can anyone say they know? Really? Maybe we're just not supposed to know.

Friday, March 13, 2009 was a typical morning outside the doors of Connecticut Superior Court at 101 Lafayette Street, a block down the street from the gold-domed state capital building. Bail bondsmen and women hawked their wares amidst a crowd of BlackBerry-connected suits, baseball-capped, heavily tattooed young men, and miscellaneous others. It was a carnival. We lined up at Mozzicato's Catering truck and at the courthouse doors guarded by metal detectors, jockeying for breakfast and justice.

So it was a relief to enter the relatively calm State's Attorney's office on the first floor, a nondescript section of the building where the Hartford area's criminal-justice activity is managed. Outside the warren of offices and cubicles, in an open central area, is a long, rectangular conference table. Before long, I was sitting there with fellow victims of the Avon

Mountain crash, those who were seriously injured or those representing loved ones who died as a result of the crash.

We were summoned by Assistant State's Attorney Dennis O'Connor, who was leading the prosecution of manslaughter and assault charges against David Wilcox. Rumor had it that Mr. Wilcox was considering some sort of plea deal.

"Oh, your SUV smashed into my minivan," said Michael Cummings to Iris Rich. "Nice to meet you."

There we were, this utterly random cross-section of society, a dozen people united by the single coincidence that we or one of our loved ones happened to approach the traffic light at the base of Avon Mountain at 7:38 a.m. on July 29, 2005.

At one point, an older gentleman with a cane and backpack limped through the office door holding a copy of the *Philadelphia Inquirer*. He was wearing a navy-blue knit hat and zippered sweatshirt. He looked uncomfortable. I would soon learn that he was Ralph Stokes, the father of Abdulraheem Naafi, the driver of Truck 8. Mr. Stokes had taken the train that morning from Philadelphia to Hartford. I had written to him a year earlier to find out more about his son, but hadn't heard back. I would soon learn more about the second oldest of his four sons.

After about 10 or 15 minutes, we were led into another office, where Mr. O'Connor took charge of the gathering. He knew everyone in the room, knew their injuries or who their loved ones were. He explained that because he was mostly finished with another high-profile case – the Windsor Locks triple homicide trial – he would now be able to focus more fully on the charges against Mr. Wilcox.

Among the things he had learned recently, he told us, was that David Wilcox was willing "to bear a heavier burden" if his wife and son were not exposed to prison sentences. More than a year ago, Donna Wilcox had pleaded no contest to insurance fraud charges. A week earlier, Shaun Wilcox pleaded guilty to tampering with evidence. They were both awaiting sentencing.

We sat quietly as Mr. O'Connor continued. His task was not easy. The atmosphere was tense. He was talking to a room full of people who had suffered enormously as a result of the Avon Mountain crash – emotionally, physically or both. The people sitting there had either been seriously injured or had collectively lost a son, husband, mother, father, sister or brother. All of us had been traumatized in some way, and none of us was happy that Mr. Wilcox had thus far escaped accountability almost four years after the crash.

The prosecutors knew crash investigators had amassed a tremendous amount of forensic evidence, and that Mr. Wilcox was sensitive to the plights of his wife and son. That knowledge helped them to negotiate a potential plea bargain, Mr. O'Connor explained. Mr. Wilcox would forego a trial and plead guilty to four counts of second-degree manslaughter, five counts of first-degree assault, and plead no contest to the insurance fraud charges. If so, the state would recommend to the sentencing judge that Donna and Shaun Wilcox should receive suspended sentences (meaning no prison time unless they violated terms of their agreements), and that David Wilcox be sentenced to 10 years in prison, suspended after six years. He would not be eligible for parole until he was almost 80 years old.

After he explained the potential plea bargain, Mr. O'Connor asked for reactions. He got them.

"He hasn't been incarcerated these past three years, and something finally can happen," said Dr. Iris Rich, one of the seriously injured. "A sentence of six years [in prison] seems bizarre – bizarre! – considering four deaths and five serious injuries. But if that's with every effort applied, that's what we ought to consider."

Mr. O'Connor thanked Dr. Rich for her comment, but there were other strong opinions to be considered.

"David, Shaun and Donna Wilcox were on the phone, conspiring about reinstating insurance retroactively and destroying evidence," said Attorney William Farrell, brother of Maureen Edlund, who was killed in the crash. "That's what they were doing while people were being carried out to the morgue." His niece, Tara Edlund, daughter of Maureen Edlund, sat by her uncle and nodded in agreement.

"He was on the phone at the site of the crash while my son was trapped in his car," said Bobbie Stotler, Chip's mom, echoing Attorney Farrell's comments.

Mr. O'Connor said his thinking had been influenced by what he had heard on different occasions over the past few years from two people who were in the room. "They both said that they wanted to see Mr. Wilcox held accountable before he leaves this earth," he said. "This deal is the best way to make sure that happens. Those people were Bobbie Stotler and Mark Robinson."

Even though the state believed it had a solid case against Mr. Wilcox, Mr. O'Connor explained, it's always a risk to go before a jury (see Chapter 14, Plodding toward Justice). And even if Mr. Wilcox was found guilty, he could appeal. That appeals process could go on for years while Mr. Wilcox remained free on bail.

Mr. O'Connor said he would explain the group's feelings to Judge David Gold at the hearing scheduled for the following Monday. He would also explain the state's case and why Mr. Wilcox was, in fact, responsible for what happened the morning of July 29, 2005.

One could only imagine what it felt like to be in the shoes of 72-year-old Ralph Stokes the morning of the meeting with Assistant State's Attorney Dennis O'Connor. He took the 5 a.m. train from his hometown of Philadelphia to represent his son, Abdulraheem Naafi, the driver of Truck 8 and one of those killed in the crash. As he sat on that train for more than three hours before arriving at Union Station in Hartford, did he wonder if the other people who would be at the meeting, people who also lost loved ones or were seriously injured, blamed his son for what happened that day?

Either way, Mr. Stokes was there for his son, the one who loved fixing bicycles as a kid playing on the streets of Philly, the one he and his wife had named Terrance. "When he was younger, he could be a little hard-headed," said Mr. Stokes, a Navy veteran and longshoreman for 35 years. "Sometimes you had to put your foot down with him, like when he would stay out late."

Never married and with no children, Abdulraheem went to computer-repair school before moving on to driving trucks. "I used to take him to Jersey where he was working, driving tractor-trailer trucks, sometimes driving cross country," Mr. Stokes said. "He loved to drive."

His son bounced around a bit and got into trouble with the law occasionally, Mr. Stokes acknowledged, but he seemed to be settling down before the crash that would claim his life. Referring to David Wilcox, Mr. Stokes said, "I can't understand how this guy could keep operating after getting all those [safety] citations." Shortly before the crash, his son called and said "'The truck is not right,'" Mr. Stokes said. "He kept sending those trucks out there. My son's life, other people's lives, were on the line."

Recent history had not been kind to the Stokes family. In addition to losing Raheem, their youngest son was shot to death in Philadelphia. "All of this has really taken a toll on my wife," said Mr. Stokes. "I had little spats with Raheem when he was younger. But when he was older, we never had any real misunderstandings. He started understanding what I told him about doing the right thing. I miss him. He was funny; most people who knew him liked him. He always had something funny to tell you. I really miss him. We all do, his brothers and sisters and nieces and nephews, we all miss him very much."

On Monday, March 16, 2009, in Connecticut Superior Court on Lafayette Street in Hartford, Conn., David Wilcox, in a sometimes barely audible voice, said the word "guilty" nine times in response to Judge David Gold's reading of the four counts of second-degree manslaughter and five counts of first-degree assault. He also pleaded no contest to insurance fraud. Sentencing was scheduled for June 24, 2009.

The River Flows On

I often think of Chip, Maureen, Bongi, Raheem and Frank. I think of them, pray for them, wish I had known them, wish they were still here with us. They were all just doing their jobs that morning, going to work to support themselves and their families. I think of the price they paid – and the unbearable price their families continue to pay – for someone else's obscene irresponsibility. It is infuriating. I can only imagine what it's like for the Stotler, Edlund, Bongiovanni, Naafi/Stokes and Juan families and friends. It is so monumentally, grotesquely unfair.

From a personal perspective, it's hard to summarize how the crash has affected me. My troubles seem almost silly and insignificant compared to those who lost loved ones. Physically, I'm basically OK. I can't bend over to tie my shoes without letting out an involuntary grunt. My back hurts once in a while. I have some aches and pains I didn't have before, possibly attributable to the now-welcome getting old factor. Or maybe it's from all those broken bones. I don't know. Psychologically, well, it's hard to say. I'm sometimes told I have survivor's guilt. Maybe so, although I'm not really sure what that means. I don't think it's unreasonable to wonder how or why one lives while others so close by died. It takes time to work through all this, which also has an effect on others. There is no doubt that tragedies affect more than just those who were directly involved. The aftershocks reverberate through many lives. I know it has helped me to talk about all this. I appreciate all those who have listened.

Sorting out the causes, consequences, what ifs and aftereffects of tragedy can take years, even lifetimes. But then, time doesn't stop; the river flows on and on. You can miss a lot by looking back. It may sound like a cliché, but a near-death experience really can inspire a deeper appreciation for life. Even so, it is all too easy as time goes on to, once again, lose perspective and get dragged under by everyday minutia. That's when I think of Chip and how, by all accounts, he had "mastered the art of living." I sometimes ask myself: How would Chip Stotler handle this situation? That's when I remember to lighten up, slow down and savor each day's gifts...my wife's sweet, lingering embrace...my son's heart-warming smile and the sound of his increasingly accomplished guitar music...the exquisite taste of Munson's chocolate...a laugh with friends and colleagues... that moment at the top of a ski slope, with all its breathtaking beauty, just before the adrenaline rush down the mountain...being part of a good team – at work, play or in community service...get-togethers with my precious family...the feel of beastie-girl Dixie's slobbering dog tongue on my right ear when I hug her warm, happy face... the pure (and increasingly rare) satisfaction of swishing a three pointer...the sound of the Beatles during those open-window summer drives to the New England shore...

I'm home. I drag a weathered park bench to the water's edge behind our Canton townhouse, probably breaking at least half a dozen condo-association rules along the way. It's late afternoon. The sun shines. The birds sing. The river flows as I listen and watch. I'm grateful, content in many ways, keenly aware of how lucky I am, how it could have ended so differently. I inhale the evergreen forest scents, feel the warm rays on my face and let the cool, clear waters of the Farmington River wash over my dangling feet as sunlight dances and sparkles on the shimmering, ever-changing surface.

EPILOGUE

One thousand, four hundred and twenty-five days after the Avon Mountain crash, David Wilcox finally faced his day of reckoning. It was June 24, 2009. The families of crash victims and Mr. Wilcox and his supporters awkwardly avoided each other in the waiting area outside a third-floor courtroom at Connecticut Superior Court in Hartford.

In a process riddled with delay, this day would be no different. We had been told that the sentencing proceeding would begin at 10 a.m. but we didn't file into the courtroom until 10:30. Thirty minutes might not seem like much, but it's an eternity when the bile and heartbreak created by an unnecessary tragedy are coursing through your veins and assaulting your gut. And then there were three other cases for Judge David P. Gold to handle before Mr. Wilcox and his attorney, Ray Hassett, took their places at the defense table.

Conspicuously placed at the center of the table was a large plastic, zip-lock bag. Clearly visible inside was a collection of prescription medicine bottles. Mr. Wilcox was said to have heart problems, diabetes and high blood pressure. So maybe he needed to keep that bag within arm's length.

But despite Mr. Wilcox's health issues, placing that bag front and center on the defense table seemed odd. Was it was a ploy, a deliberate defense tactic, an attempt to gain sympathy for the man who was within a few weeks of his 74th birthday? If so, the tactic was about to backfire.

During one break between cases, Bobbie Stotler and my wife, Chris, went to the ladies room. Bobbie told Chris she was frustrated with the delays and that she was nervous, that she wasn't sure she could stand in front of the court and say what she wanted to say. This was a woman who had endured so much – the sudden and shocking death of her cherished first-born son, the father of five of her young granddaughters, the brother of her younger daughter and son, the husband of her daughter-in-law. Bobbie's suffering had taken a serious toll on her health. Through it all, she had carried herself with incredible grace, dignity and courage, earning the deep admiration and respect of all who knew her.

When the time came, Bobbie walked to the front of the courtroom and stood straight and tall. After nearly four years of waiting, her moment had arrived, and Bobbie Stotler delivered. She looked over at the defense table and said, "Before the crash, I was in perfect health. Now I have a medicine bag three times bigger than that one."

She turned back to face Judge Gold. "How can I share with you my pain?" she said. "Could you tolerate the rawness of my heartache? My task is to tell you about one very special life that was so callously ended by David Wilcox." Bobbie then went on to talk about Chip and what a great person he was, about how he adored his family, about how everyone adored him, about the effect his death has had on them. She talked about his last moments.

"While my son was alive and lucid, and while my son died, David Wilcox was nearby on his cell phone," she said. "I was told that a stranger at the scene [West Hartford Police Officer Rob Magao] crawled into the wreckage of my son's car to help keep my son alive and to hold his hand and offer comfort. This man said that Chip was totally lucid and expressed concern for that person's safety, telling him to leave and get himself some help. The kind stranger stayed with him. Chip's last moment was spent worrying about the people he loved. During those last few moments, David Wilcox showed complete disregard and lack of concern for the human suffering he had caused...

"It has been almost four years since the accident," Bobbie continued. "David Wilcox has been free and out on bond through his stalling and denying tactics...he belongs in jail. He belonged in jail since the beginning. He has shown absolutely no remorse. I again implore you to sentence him to the maximum sentence possible. It will be a touch of justice for the victims.

"I will miss Chip every day of my life," Bobbie said. "I will hold him in my heart forever."

Once again, I had watched in awe as Bobbie Stotler stood up for her son and her entire family. I was also deeply moved by the statements of Tara Edlund, whose mother Maureen was killed in the crash, and her uncle, Bill Farrell, Maureen's brother.

Tara talked of her upcoming July wedding. Her father had died when she was nine. With her beloved mother's death, neither parent would be there to witness her marriage to Andrew Scott. She described her mother as her best friend, her confidante, her "first phone call" when she had something – anything, good or bad – to share. When new acquaintances wished her and Andrew well, saying that her mother must be enjoying the wedding preparations, Tara would have to explain the heart-breaking reality that her mother was deceased.

It was then her uncle's turn. He held up a picture of his sister, Tara's mom, and told the defense that her name was Maureen Edlund, not "victim number two." According to the *Hartford Courant*, "William Farrell...expressed disgust at what he saw as Wilcox's lack of remorse. Farrell also had a word on behalf of [Truck 8 driver Abdulraheem] Naafi, who died a horrible death as fire consumed the truck. In the immediate aftermath of the crash, Wilcox and his lawyers laid blame for the crash on Naafi and even suggested he intentionally crashed the truck and may have been a terrorist."[1]

As far as I know, those lawyers never offered any evidence to support those shameful comments. At the very least, they should apologize to Raheem's family.

Michael Juan and Ramona Clark spoke for their father, Frank Juan. Floyd Amicone was there to speak for his sister, Barbara Bongiovanni. And then a letter from Raheem's father, Ralph Stokes, who was not able to be in court this day, was read out loud.

"For those of us who have lost a loved one, the loss is never ending," Mr. Stokes had written. "For those who suffered serious bodily injuries, their pain will last for as long as they live. We are all still suffering years after the crime was committed. He has not even begun to pay his debt, and now we know he will only serve six years in jail. His suffering will end – ours will not. Six years for altering the lives of at least 20 people does not seem sufficient in my eyes or those of my wife, Brenda."

Then it was my turn to speak. I briefly considered passing on the opportunity. My troubles paled in comparison to those who lost loved ones. And saying more at this point almost felt like "piling on." At the same time, I didn't want to look back with any "would've, could've, should've" feelings. Also, there was at least one additional point to be made. So I went forward and read a brief statement that I had prepared in advance.

After mentioning Chip, Maureen, Barbara, Frank and Raheem – and saying the depth of this tragedy could not be understood unless you knew who they were – I said, "Judge Gold, nothing we do here today will bring them back. All we can do is honor their memories and lessen the chance that another uninsured, wretchedly maintained truck will blast more innocent lives apart. I urge you to hold Mr. Wilcox accountable, and to send a clear message to any other owners out there who would try to save a few bucks while running their businesses in such an incredibly irresponsible way."

Wilcox's Turn

Now it was time for David Wilcox to stand up and address the court. He was free to say virtually anything. It was his chance to explain his version of what had happened and his feelings about that. His defense attorney, Ray Hassett, spoke first.

He said that his client was "deeply and profoundly sorry for everything that has occurred." Mr. Hassett also took the blame for any perceived lack of remorse on Mr. Wilcox's part, explaining that as his attorney, he had advised Mr. Wilcox not to talk about the case.

Now it was finally time for Mr. Wilcox to speak. He at times had buried

---

1. *Hartford Courant*, June 25, 2009, "Trucking Company Owner Sentenced to Six Years for 2005 Avon Crash," David Owens and Christine Dempsey

his head in his hands and cried. There was no joy in watching his misery. It was a sad situation, but a situation that Mr. Wilcox himself had created. All sympathy belonged to those who lost loved ones. I couldn't help but wonder if Mr. Wilcox was feeling sorry for what he was responsible for, or just sorry for himself.

He struggled to get to his feet, and then he took a long, deep breath. After a pause, he tapped Mr. Hassett's shoulder and whispered, "Could you read this?" Mr. Hassett read the words on the sheet of paper Mr. Wilcox had handed him, words that included: "I'm sorry for what happened...It was a terrible accident. If there was something I could do to take away what happened that day, I would."

All eyes then turned to Judge Gold. It had been almost four years since Mr. Wilcox's Truck 8 had barreled down Avon Mountain and devastated the lives of so many. The days between the crash and this day's sentencing were filled with anger, tears, heartache, unanswerable questions, raw pain and frustration. How would the judge handle the overwhelming task before him?

Judge Gold clearly had given this moment much thought. He said he could not do what the victims' families really wanted, which was to turn back the hands of time and bring their loved ones back. He explained some of the difficult particulars of this case, including the fact that intent was a factor he was obligated to consider. After all, no one was accusing Mr. Wilcox of waking up the morning of July 29, 2005 and deliberately setting out to kill five people.

At the same time, however, what happened was "no accident" but rather a "virtual certainty" given the way Mr. Wilcox had run his business, Judge Gold said. "You made a series of intentional and volitional choices that joined together to form this perfect storm that led to the Route 44 disaster." His focus was not on keeping the truck truly roadworthy and safe, but merely operational.

"Closing your eyes to the danger was not significantly different than getting in, turning the key, closing your eyes and driving it," Judge Gold told Mr. Wilcox. "You knew that truck had problems with the brakes, tires and transmission."

Judge Gold then mentioned a metaphor I had used in a victim's impact letter I had sent him a week before the sentencing. "I continue to be haunted by the fact that this tragedy was so preventable," I had written. "David Wilcox played Russian roulette with all of us for many years. According to his arrest warrant affidavit, he had 1,136 safety violations. The investigation found that his Truck 8 had a total of 20 pre-crash equipment violations including mismatched brake chambers, misadjusted brakes, oversized brake drums, contaminated brake linings, a defective brake slack adjuster and an inoperative parking brake."

Judge Gold extended the Russian roulette metaphor, saying that rather than placing just one bullet in one of the gun's chambers and leaving the other five empty, Mr. Wilcox had, in effect, put bullets in every single chamber. One major difference, the judge said, was that people who play this game presumably know they're in a life-and-death situation. The people waiting in their vehicles at the base of Avon Mountain July 29, 2005 had no idea they were involved in a deadly game.

"You played Russian roulette that day with everybody who came near that truck," Judge Gold said. "The only one not playing was you."

In the end, Judge Gold sentenced Mr. Wilcox to six years in prison, the maximum allowed under a deal he had made with prosecutors in exchange for guilty pleas to four counts of second-degree manslaughter, five counts of first-degree assault, and a no-contest plea to a single count of insurance fraud.

Given the circumstances, I thought Judge Gold did a good job. He was thoughtful and thorough in his explanations. I believe that he listened to the victims and had a good understanding of what they had endured. While I had been frustrated with the many delays and benefits extended to Mr. Wilcox at the expense of the victims, I was grateful for the way Judge Gold handled the sentencing.

Going Forward

There has been a tremendous outpouring of sympathy for the victims of the Avon Mountain crash. I know how much I appreciate all the kind gestures. But some victims continue to face severe financial challenges as a direct result of what happened that day. More should be done for them.

The State of Connecticut, in particular, should do more – much more – because it bears a significant portion of responsibility for the Avon Mountain crash. As detailed earlier in this book, it enabled David Wilcox by:

- Creating a loophole in the 1993 legislation intended to get uninsured motorists off the road by explicitly exempting commercial entities, a loophole Mr. Wilcox repeatedly exploited (the loophole was eliminated shortly after the crash);

- Giving Mr. Wilcox $1.6 million of business at the same time it cited him with 1,136 safety violations;

- Not moving faster to make Avon Mountain safer – Mr. Wilcox's Truck 8 was the seventh truck in 21 years to lose its brakes descending the mountain; it took the eighth truck in 23 years, the one that crashed into Nassau's Furniture store on Sept. 7, 2007, before the state took decisive corrective action, i.e., building a runaway truck ramp and making significant road improvements.

The good news is that the State of Connecticut waived tuition fees at state colleges for children of those who were killed in the Avon Mountain crash. But it needs to do more. A headline in the Aug. 24, 2009 edition of Time magazine read, "Raising a Child Costs Some $221,000, *Before* College." And tuition at top-tier, out-of-state schools currently totals approximately $200,000 for four years for one student. Beyond post-high school education expenses, some families are also dealing with the aftermath of not only losing a cherished loved one, but also losing the income the loved one contributed to their families.

In addition, I urge the lawmakers who expressed outrage and concern for the victims after the crash to do the right thing. They can't bring back Chip Stotler, Maureen Edlund, Barbara Bongiovanni, Abdulraheem Naafi and Frank Juan, but they can make sure their families are not suffering financially due to a tragedy the state could have prevented. Minnesota legislators did the right thing in the aftermath of the Aug. 1, 2007 bridge collapse in Minneapolis. Within a year of that tragedy, the families of the 13 people who were killed were provided with at least some financial relief. Connecticut legislators should do the same. Also, our legislators can also continue to work to ensure that the conditions that contributed to the Avon Mountain tragedy are greatly reduced and, where possible, eliminated.

As for the rest of us, we must work with our elected officials and law enforcement to help make our roads safer. Perhaps the single most important factor in achieving that goal is for all of us to drive more carefully, more patiently, more sanely. All the road safety improvements in the world are not enough to overcome bad driving and poorly maintained vehicles.

Finally, we can continue to summon "the better angels of our nature" by keeping the spirit of the Avon Mountain rescuers alive. When confronted with catastrophe, they embraced the chance to help their fellow human beings. To quote the the inspiring words of Dr. William Petit, we need to go forward "with the inclination to live with a faith that embodies action: Help a neighbor, fight for a cause, love your family."

ACKNOWLEDGEMENTS

Soon after the Avon Mountain crash, I knew I wanted to write a book about it. My goal was to have the book ready for distribution by the first anniversary of the crash. I was off by more than three years. Looking back, I had no idea of what I was getting into. I needed help to get this project done. Time and time again, in one way or another, people stepped up to provide that help. I am deeply grateful.

In one sense, this entire book is a thank-you note. There are so many to thank, from the rescuers who risked their lives to all those who sent cards, food, plants and flowers. Thank you to everyone. I was overwhelmed. I never understood how powerful a simple note could be until I was flat on my back for a few weeks. My wife, Chris, saved the cards and letters I received after the crash. I just reread them after I finished writing the epilogue, and was touched all over again by all the kind wishes.

I apologize in advance to those whose names I will undoubtedly remember right after I send the final manuscript to the printer.

Thank you to all those who took such great care of me after the crash, including Kyle Caruso, Doug Smith, Lai Shawn Hooks, Tom Clynch, Victor Morrone, Todd Jensen, Mike Gulino, Tony Flamio, Patient Care Assistant Victor Rivera, Dr. Scott Kurtzman, Dr. Ron Gross, Dr. Gerald Becker, Dr. Kevin Burton, Dr. Arun Mavanur, Dr. John D'Avella, Patty Frasier and the Hartford Hospital ICU and Stepdown Unit nurses, and my wife, Chris.

Thank you to all the fire safety, law enforcement and emergency services people, including Peter Agnesi, David Bourque, John Chevalier, Pete Delap, Jamie DiPace, Charles Epstein and the Critical Incident Team, Jeff Hogan, Sue Kassey, Rob Magao, Todd Myers, Jason Reid, Mark Rinaldo, Mark Samsel, Tim Vibert, Jon Widing, Russ Wininger, the LifeStar flight crews, and the entire North Central Municipal Accident Reconstruction Squad.

Thank you to the anonymous endocrinologist, who helped at least one seriously injured driver at the crash and then quietly left before anyone could thank him. He represents all the people who came to the rescue the day of the crash to help their fellow human beings.

Thank you to the families of those who died in the crash, and to those who were seriously injured, for giving me the privilege of sharing their stories with me. This book could not have been done without their help. I especially want to thank Bobbie Stotler, Lori (Stotler) McGarrahan, John Stotler, Joe Grieco, Tara (Edlund) Scott, Vincent Bongiovanni, Floyd Amicone, Ralph Stokes, the Juan family, Elena Tomasi and Michael Cummings.

Thank you to the people who provided tremendous support with this project's editing, photography, design, marketing, promotion, production and distribution, including Chris John Amorosino, John Muldoon, Mary Crombie, Howard Drescher, Jeff Dornenburg, Elizabeth Cowles, Eric Tully, Barbara Barry, Beth Bruno, Nancy Simonds, Sue Apito, Brian Jud, John Drewry, Michelle Leibovitz, Rich Wright, Darcy O'Connor, Jeff Paine, Gery Krewson, and the Avon Fire and Police Department photographers.

Thank you to those who endorsed this book. When asked, they embraced the chance to help Avon Mountain crash victims. Thank you to Coach Jim Calhoun, Jerry Franklin, Tom McInerney, Dr. William Petit, Diane Smith and Bruce Stevens, all of whom could not have been more gracious and helpful.

Thank you to my employer, ING, for its support. Virtually all companies talk about being responsible corporate citizens and supporting their employees. ING backs its words with actions. That may be because it employs so many really good people. I want to thank all the past and present ING employees who wished me well, including Carol Albanese, Carolyn Armitage, Kim Audia, Stacy Bagby, Randy Bailin, Steve Baskin, Claudia Bateman, Terri Bellobuono, Marianne Bendoraitis, Dianne Bernez, Linda "LB" Biancalani, Linda Segal Blinn, Jeoff Block, Trish Bock, Jane Boyle, Shelley Brooks, Kevin Brown, Valerie Brown, Stacy Brusa, Gale Busemeyer, Rachel Camargo, Karen Christman, Christine Cloud, Tracey Coleman, Sue Collins, Tricia Conahan, Shauna Corley, Terry Crean, Bob Crispin, Judith Cummings, Connie Cunningham, Serena Deets, Rhondalee Deschamps, Barb Deubel, Jim Dolan, Tracey Eck, Michael Eldredge, Janice Ewers, Ron Falkner, Janna Fenwick, Jackie Figliola, Susan Forsdick, JoAnn Galvin, Betsy Gentile, Jack Goulet, Joe Grieco, Brian Haendiges, Denise Hamar, Cynthia Hamel, Lorna Hamilton, Debbie Herman, Toby Hoden, Laura Holm, Denise Jackson, Jen Jordan, Maureen Kelly, Pam Kursman, Ed Kushner, Bob Leghorn, Sharon Malone, Nan Marjama, Shaun Mathews, Tom McInerney, Larry Milan, John Montaro, Kathy Murphy, Venkata Natarajan, Maureen Parker, Karen Parks, Cisaltina Pina, Tom Porell, Ginette Purcell, Sri Reddy, Kim Renehan, Charlene Rioux-Davis, Jacqui Robertson, Lynne Rogers, Tracey Roosland, Linda Rutkauskas, Trish Sarno, Lisa Scalise, Bev Seaver, Mila Shafir, Susan Shaw, Dave Sheridan, Catherine Smith, Sandy Collins Smith, Donna Speziale, Jana Stern, Kathleen Stone, Marie Stuart, Joann Swan, Amy Vaillancourt, Tim Varriale, Camille Villaver, Tom Waldron, Margaret Wall, Donna Westman, Micki Wildin, Judeen Wrinn and Barbara Zoghbi; all my fellow ING Orange Toast Toastmasters; and all my ING communications colleagues including Sofia Almeida, Kim Arculeo, Lisette Boer, Tom Collins, Christina Divigard, Chuck Eudy, Kristie Grieve, Allan Jaeger, Christy Kane, Jeremy Litton, Joe Loparco, Phil Margolis, Jennifer Matticks, Darcy O'Connor, Jeffrey

Peebles, Adena Puchalski, Dana Ripley, Tom Schnetz, Ward Snijders, Bill Spiers, Teko Verheijen, Karen Wassell, and Ruth Weber Kelley

Thank you to my "old" Security-Connecticut Life and ReliaStar friends, including Angela Arnott, Anita Blood, Bob Bomgaars, Tom Boyd, Pat DeVita, Mark Dymersky, Laurie Fall, Tammy Felciano, Dan Ferrante, Charlene Fischler, Paul Garofoli, Jim Gelder, Bob Gerrett, Maureen Gitschier, Ruth Grant, Vicki Hack, Val Hayes, Laura and Steve Holtzman, Ron Jarvis, Nicki Jud, Joyce Kerr, Joan Kinsley, Cindy Knox, Tina Leone, Dave Lejeune, Joanne Marhefki, Traci McIntyre, Randy Miller, Joan Muldoon-Burk, Karen Nadeau, Ann O'Brien, Carol OJ, Lynn Pellegrini, Helen Piechocki, Marianne Rice, Corriene Rozzi, Beth Rusnock, Betsy Turbacuski, Marlene Snell, Peter and Laurie Susi, and Sue Wood.

Thank you my "old" Travelers friends, including Walt Cherniak, Howard Drescher, Jim Kalach, John (and Brian) Legere, Dennis Milewski, Rosemary O'Neill, Doug Quat, Damien Roohr, Sam Stuart and Deb Susca.

Thank you to those who provided help and advice on finance, legal and political issues, including Carole Briggs, Maura Kehoe Coyne, Louis DeLuca, John Droney, Patrick Flaherty, Linda Johnston, Ken Levine, John Malone, Priya Morganstern, Dennis O'Connor, Pat Perfetto, Phil Schenck, Paul Skripol, John Todd and Adriana Venegas.

Thank you to those who shared their expertise about truck mechanics and safety, especially Jack Matava, Chip Mowrey, Andy Romano and Phillip Wilson.

Thank you to those who opened doors for me and helped me find information, including Susan Dalgleish, Chip Geer, Mike Gessford, Nancy Green, Prenzina Holloway, Nora Howard, Elissa Kiessling, Kristen Loparco, Bobbie-Ann Marquis, Justin McGlamery, Yvette Melling, John Norman, LeRoy Pittman, Chick Pritchard, Mike Riley, Katie Robidoux, Jon Warren, the Office of Legislative Research and librarians at the Avon Public Library and the Connecticut State Library, Law/Legislative Reference Unit.

Thank you to my Coventry friends, including Barbara Barry, Patrick Flaherty, Butch and Patti Fleeher, Betty Peracchio and all my friends at Second Congregational Church; and to Bobbi and Jack Bynes, and Kathy Ryan.

Thank you to my "old" Brewster friends, including Roger Aylward, Roseanne (DiNardo) Galante, Tom Malone, Ann McCarthy, Kate McCarthy, Deb and John McCarthy, Sister Maureen McMahon, and Jackie and Joe Quinn.

Thank you to the current and former members (and spouses) of St. Mary Star of the Sea's adult choir, Two or More (contemporary singing group) and parish members, including the Bonini family, Keith Jakobowski, Judy Welcome and most especially Father John Golas – for their prayers, flowers, Mass cards and well wishes. A special thanks to Presbyterian Church of Coventry for including me in their prayers, and to Harvest Fellowship Church in Springfield, Mass. for including Maureen Edlund and me on its prayer list.

Thank you for the support I received from my friends at the Valley Fitness Center, including Gerry Cote and Phyllis Kelleher, Sue and Doug Davenport, Jeff Hogan, Mike Mansour, Marc Saillant and Andre Szychowski.

Thank you to our Unionville and Canton neighbors, including Barbara Backman, Marygale Bouldin, Mary and Tom Downs, Fran Festa, Doris Hayward, Nancy Hogan, Claudia Lampert, Alice Lund, Mary Ellen Massicotte, Clee and Warren Priest, Elizabeth and John Norman, Grace and Dave Sharp, Shari Tomko, Maryellen Welcome, and Janice Williams and Rob Bell.

My wife, Chris, would like to extend a big thank you for the tremendous outpouring of support she has received, including her friends at Farmington Town Hall for their well wishes, cards, flowers, baked goods, gift cards and continued support – you will never know how much it meant to her; to her fellow C.C.M.C. colleagues; to Geno Avenoso and the staff at Franklin Jewelers; to Maryann Douglas, Linda Nadeau, John and Joan Narkiewicz, Marie Parady and Diane Rogers; to Coach Chris's 'soccer girls' – a big thank you for caring about her; to the Unionville Friendly's crew; to Chris's Mom's friends and colleagues at Simsbury Town Hall; to her sister Mary's friends; to her volleyball friends; to all those who sent flowers – Sue and Chris Duhaime, Maureen Jessen and Janet Goman, Susan Kelly, Sophie Sawicki and Paul and Roberta Skripol; to those who sent fruit arrangements and made countless dinners, including Ray and Tracy Beloin, Donna and Jon LeBlanc, Diane and John Lipari and Elva Stregowski – your kindness will never be forgotten; to the wonderful women of the Farmington Junior Women's Club, a huge thank you for the beach bag filled with goodies and books that kept Chris distracted while she spent hours with me at the hospital; and to Chris's sister Mary and her Mom, Helen, along with her very dear friends – especially Marygale Bouldin, Cheryl Briere, Wendy Ceccucci, Karin Comer, Carol and Jeff Hall, Lori Kipperman, Donna LeBlanc, Anne Lemke – your love has meant the world to her.

Thank you to members of the media for helping to tell the Avon Mountain story, including Shawn Beals, Debra Bogstie, Frank Borres, Jacqueline Bennett, Katishia Cosley, Christine Dempsey, Ray Dunaway, Dan Jones, Tracy Kennedy, Katie Melone, Matt Negrin, David Owens, Natalie Pollock, Brigitte Ruthman, Diane Smith, Bruce Stevens, Tricia Taskey and Bob Wilson.

ACKNOWLEDGEMENTS

Thank you to all those who provided editorial advice including Chris John Amorosino, Roger Aylward, Linda "LB" Biancalani, Beth Bruno, Tom Collins, Howard Drescher, Chuck Eudy, Charlene Fischler, Doris Kearns Goodwin, Stan Gorzelany, Jr., Joe Grieco, Kristie Grieve, Brian Haendiges, Valerie Jacobs, Donna and Jon LeBlanc, Nancy Simonds, Sam Stuart, Deb Susca and Ruth Weber Kelley.

Thank you to our family, including Matt, Dixie, Ken, Paul and Heather (and Tim, Jack and Julie), Nancy and Stan (and Kevin and Annie), the McKenney family, Helen, Mary, Bill (and Mikala and Rachel), Joe, Norma, Bill, Lisa, Leslie and Nick (and Hannah and Katelyn), Joan, Rev. Raymond Nugent, Gloria and Roger, Matt, Michelle, Paul and Sheri, Mark and Cheryl – thanks for taking care of Dixie while I was in the hospital! – and Robert and Diane, Eileen and Bill, and Richard and Eileen.

Thank you to the generous donors whose contributions ensured the production of *Smoke, Fire and Angels*. Thank you to ING, Duncan Somerville, Stan and Nancy McKenney, and Bob Switzgable and Ski Sundown.

I am profoundly grateful. Thank you all very, very much!!!

RESOURCES

The businesses that helped create *Smoke, Fire and Angels* and guide and/
or contribute to its marketing and promotional efforts include:

Acorn Studio, Glastonbury, Conn.;
www.acornstudio.biz

Amorosino Writing, Unionville, Conn.;
www.amorosinowriting.com

BHB Mailing Services, Coventry, Conn.;
www.bhbmailing.com

Beth Bruno, Book Editing Associates;
www.book-editing.com/bios/beth-bruno

Dornenburg Group, West Hartford, Conn.;
www.dornenburg.com

The Kotchen Group, Farmington, Conn.;
www.kotchengroup.com

Lasting Image New Media, Hartford, Conn.;
www.lastingimage.com

Levy & Droney, P.C., Farmington, Conn.;
www.ldlaw.com

Muldoon Photography, Farmington, Conn.;
www.muldoonphoto.com

Nancy Simonds Communication, South Windsor, Conn.;
www.simonds.com

Rich Wright Productions, West Springfield, Mass.;
www.richwrightproductions.com